Inclusive Education for Learners with Multisensory Impairment

Inclusive Education for Learners with Multisensory Impairment

Best Practices and Research Priorities

Leda Kamenopoulou

Open University Press

Open University Press
McGraw Hill
Unit 4
Foundation Park
Roxborough Way
Maidenhead
SL6 3UD

email: emea_uk_ireland@mheducation.com
world wide web: www.mheducation.co.uk

Copyright © Open International Publishing Limited, 2023

All rights reserved. Except for the quotation of short passages for the purposes of criticism and review, no part of this publication may be reproduced, stored in a retrieval system, or transmitted, in any form or by any means, electronic, mechanical, photocopying, recording or otherwise, without the prior written permission of the publisher or a licence from the Copyright Licensing Agency Limited. Details of such licences (for reprographic reproduction) may be obtained from the Copyright Licensing Agency Ltd of Saffron House, 6–10 Kirby Street, London EC1N 8TS.

Executive Editor: Eleanor Christie
Editorial Assistant: Zoe Osman
Content Product Manager: Ali Davis

A catalogue record of this book is available from the British Library

ISBN-13: 9780335249671
ISBN-10: 0335249671
eISBN: 9780335249688

Library of Congress Cataloging-in-Publication Data
CIP data applied for

Typeset by Transforma Pvt. Ltd., Chennai, India

Fictitious names of companies, products, people, characters and/or data that may be used herein (in case studies or in examples) are not intended to represent any real individual, company, product or event.

Praise page

"This is a welcome and much needed addition to the literature of sensory impairment and education. Multisensory impairment is a unique disability which is associated with a unique range of needs and educational requirements. In this clearly structured book, Leda Kamenopoulou offers a useful analysis of theories that can most usefully capture this, and offers guidance on important educational responses and interventions. The book offers a broad and helpful definition of inclusive education – one which centres upon high quality, relevant and evidenced teaching and support."
Graeme Douglas, Professor of Disability and Special Educational Needs, University of Birmingham, UK

"This book is a must-have for every teacher in primary and secondary schools and should be compulsory literature on all teacher training courses. Leda Kamenopoulou has succeeded in showcasing her in depth knowledge in a concise way, making the book accessible to a broad group of educators such as teachers, caregivers, parents, and all other professionals responsible for the supervision of learners with MSI. As there is so much work to be done in this area, this book will help to raise awareness among all teachers, for only then can the needs of MSI students be supported."
Marleen J. Janssen, Ph.D., Professor Inclusive and Special Needs Education, University of Groningen Institute for Deafblindness, The Netherlands

This book is dedicated to Dr Olga Miller, my doctoral thesis supervisor, who generously welcomed me to her academic family almost 20 years ago, and not only taught me a lot about multisensory impairment, but also gave me a true masterclass on how to be a good supervisor – for which reason I will forever be grateful to her, and I am sure all my students will feel the same.

Contents

List of tables	xi
List of acronyms	xii
Acknowledgements	xiv
Foreword	xv
Preface	xvii

CHAPTER 1: INTRODUCTION — 1
1.1 Book focus, rationale and objectives — 1
1.2 What is multisensory impairment? — 2
    1.2.1 Definition and terminology — 2
    1.2.2 Prevalence — 4
1.3 What is inclusive education? — 6
    1.3.1 International context: the inclusion agenda and its challenges — 6
    1.3.2 The argument: Why is this book necessary? — 9
1.4 Overview of chapters — 11

CHAPTER 2: RESEARCH: REVIEW OF THE LITERATURE — 13
2.1 Cautionary note on reviewing the literature on MSI — 13
2.2 Brief historical overview — 14
    2.2.1 Early pioneering work in the US — 14
    2.2.2 Early pioneering work in the Soviet Union — 15
    2.2.3 The late twentieth century: work in the Netherlands, UK and US — 18
2.3 Research in the twenty-first century: across the globe — 24
    2.3.1 England and the UK — 25
    2.3.2 International — 37
2.4 Concluding notes — 42

CHAPTER 3: THEORY: MSI AND CHILD DEVELOPMENT — 43
3.1 Factors affecting the impact of MSI on development — 43
3.2 Impact on child development: primary difficulties — 43
3.3 Impact on child development: secondary difficulties — 45
3.4 Useful theoretical perspectives — 46
    3.4.1 Attachment theory and MSI — 47
    3.4.2 Social learning, deprivation theories and MSI — 48
    3.4.3 Sociocultural theory and MSI — 50
    3.4.4 Summary of useful theoretical approaches — 51
3.5 Bioecological systems theory — 52
    3.5.1 Bioecological systems theory and MSI — 53
    3.5.2 Benefits and challenges of bioecological systems theory — 56
3.6 Summary of impact on development and implications for education — 58

CHAPTER 4: PRACTICE: EDUCATIONAL STRATEGIES — 59
- 4.1 MSI, educational implications, and areas of need — 59
- 4.2 Educational strategies — 63
  - 4.2.1 Developing communication — 63
  - 4.2.2 Access and independence — 71
  - 4.2.3 Teaching style — 73
  - 4.2.4 Building world knowledge — 77
  - 4.2.5 Nurturing peer relationships — 80
- 4.3 General considerations — 84
  - 4.3.1 Listening to children and young people — 84
  - 4.3.2 The value of observation and reflective practice — 87
  - 4.3.3 Brief note about the curriculum — 90
- 4.4 Illustrative case studies — 90
  - 4.4.1 Case study 1: Aisha — 91
  - 4.4.2 Case study 2: Adel — 92
  - 4.4.3 Case study 3: Frank — 93
  - 4.4.4 Case study 4: Elena — 94
- 4.5 Summary — 95

CHAPTER 5: FUTURE DIRECTIONS IN RESEARCH, THEORY AND PRACTICE — 97
- 5.1 Research: what do we need to explore better or more? — 97
- 5.2 Theory: what do we need to think about better or more? — 99
- 5.3 Practice: what do we need to do better or more? — 101

Appendix: Useful websites — 104

References — 108

Index — 121

List of tables

Table 2.1:	Early pioneering work in the US: key learning points	15
Table 2.2:	Early pioneering work in the Soviet Union: Meshcheryakov key learning points	18
Table 2.3:	Late twentieth century: key learning points	24
Table 2.4:	Research in the twenty-first century in England: key learning points	36
Table 2.5:	International research in the twenty-first century: key learning points	41
Table 4.1:	Educational strategies for learners with MSI	62
Table 4.2:	Overview of strategy: 'developing communication'	63
Table 4.3:	Activity: Developing communication	69
Table 4.4:	Evidence-based practice sheet	70
Table 4.5:	Overview of strategy: 'access and independence'	71
Table 4.6:	Activity: Exploring Access (1)	74
Table 4.7:	Activity: Exploring Access (2)	74
Table 4.8:	Overview of strategy: 'teaching style'	75
Table 4.9:	Activity: Comparing MSI with single sensory impairment (SSI)	77
Table 4.10:	Overview of strategy: 'building world knowledge'	78
Table 4.11:	Activity: 'Hand over Hand' or 'hand under hand'?	80
Table 4.12:	Overview of strategy: 'nurturing peer relationships'	81
Table 4.13:	Activity: Streaming by ability as a practice	83
Table 4.14:	Summary of tips for enabling children to share their views	86
Table 4.15:	Activity: Involving children with complex needs in research	87
Table 4.16:	Activity: Developing and using an observation schedule for MSI	88

List of acronyms

AAC	alternative and augmentative communication
ADHD	attention deficit hyperactivity disorder
ASD	autistic spectrum disorder
AV	auditory verbal
BSL	British Sign Language
BST	bioecological systems theory
CIE	Centre for Inclusive Education
CHARGE	Coloboma of the eye, Heart defects, Atresia of the choanae, Restriction of Growth, Ear abnormalities and deafness
CLDD	complex learning difficulties and disabilities
CP	communication portfolio
DoH	Department of Health
EHCP	education, health and care plan
EST	ecological systems theory
GEM	global education monitoring [report]
HACs	human aids to communication
HI	hearing impairment
IEP	individual education plan
ICF	International Classification of Functioning
IOE, UCL	Institute of Education, University College London
LD	learning disability
LEAs	local education authorities
LSAs	learning support assistants
LVAs	low vision aids
MD	multiple disabilities
MDVI	multiple disabilities and vision impairment
MOVE	Mobility Opportunities Via Education
MSE	multisensory environment
MSI	multisensory impairment
PE	physical exercise
PECS	Picture Exchange Communication System

PMD	profound multiple disabilities
QTVI	qualified teacher for the visually impaired
QTHI	qualified teacher for the hearing impaired
RNIB	Royal National Institute for the Blind
TEACCH	Treatment and Education of Autistic and related Communication Handicapped Children
SEN/D	special educational needs/disabilities
SEN/DCO	special educational needs/disabilities coordinator
SDG(s)	sustainable development goal(s)
S/PMLD	severe/profound and multiple learning difficulty/disability
SR	sensory room
SSI	single sensory impairment
TA	teaching assistant
UD	Universal Design
UDL	Universal Design for Learning
UNCRC	United Nations Convention on the Rights of the Child
UNCRPD	United Nations Convention on the Rights of Persons with Disabilities
UNESCO	United Nations Educational, Scientific and Cultural Organization
VI	vision impairment
WHO	World Health Organization
ZPD	zone of proximal development

Acknowledgements

I have many people to thank for supporting, encouraging and inspiring me during the writing of this book. I could never have done it without my awesome colleagues at the Department of Psychology and Human Development, IOE, UCL's Faculty of Education and Society cheering me along the way. I owe thanks especially to Professor Chloë Marshall for always asking how my book was going, for being keen to talk about 'meta-strategies' and for sharing her wisdom. Dr Jessica Hayton deserves a very special mention, for generously helping me clarify my understanding of the notion of sensory processing difficulties and for exchanging ideas about teaching activities. A special thanks to my Head of Department, Dr Zachary Walker, who kept reminding me to 'go back to writing' but also to have a rest when I was feeling overwhelmed.

I am also thankful to Zoë Osman, editorial assistant at Open University Press, for all her help and support, and to the anonymous peer reviewer, for their enthusiastic comments and constructive feedback to earlier drafts of the manuscript that helped improve it considerably.

I would like to thank my family, especially my beloved parents, Marina and Kostis; my yiayia, Georgia, for always passionately believing in me; and my husband, Leonardo, particularly for his culinary skills! Last but not least, I owe a massive thanks to my gorgeous, funny, kind and bright children, Marcelo and Elektra, for understanding that 'No, I haven't finished working yet, I am still writing', and for being really patient with me during this entire year – my besties, SAS AGAPAO to the moon and back, and yes, we did it!

Dr Leda Kamenopoulou
London, April 2022

Foreword

Multisensory impairment (MSI) is considered a 'minority within a minority' of people with sensory impairment. Though causes vary between congenital and acquired forms of hearing and vision impairment, total dual sensory loss (vision and hearing) is remarkably rare. Drawing upon published works from a global perspective, this book aligns (surprisingly common) misconceptions regarding definitions of MSI, capturing historical and contemporary understandings. The underpinning literature and theory are expertly curated, culminating in practical, salient, strategies and future directions for research and practitioners. Peppered with personal commentary and case studies, a human understanding of a real-world phenomenon is presented in an approachable and meaningful way.

'Inclusion' is a term used in special educational needs and/or disabilities, often as a buzzword, so organizations do not fall foul of external scrutiny. Meaning that 'inclusion' can be superficial, transient, or more likely, ad hoc additions to existing structures, labelled as 'inclusive' when reality differs. One central premise of the book is encouraging and listening to the voices of the 'minority within the minority', children with MSI, to ensure their bespoke needs are not lost among other groups considered 'easier' to include. The book in/directly places responsibility on decision-makers involved in MSI provision, ensuring their attention prioritizes the *quality* of education and participation, as opposed to the 'placement' of the child. Emphasizing participation rather than location, is fundamental in including all children, particularly those with MSI and their families, in planning. This is a gentle yet powerful reminder to ensure the voices of children with MSI are heard and *listened to* in respect of their learning arrangements, and a call to arms ensuring that educators are adequately prepared and trained to support individualized needs.

Underpinning theory is central to understanding practice. The complex interaction between the developing child and the people/objects in their environment, is essential to understanding and tailoring provision. Medical and social models of disability influence theoretical perspectives. While Chapter 3 acknowledges the assumptions of both models, the application of the bioecological systems theory and capability approach offers a firm basis for understanding child development in the context of MSI. The combination of the theories challenges the reader in conceptualizing how a child with MSI can both understand their environment and initiate/inhibit appropriate action given familiar and unfamiliar scenarios. Accommodating the biological, psychological and social needs of the child, the approach considers modification of the environment to adapt to individualized, bespoke needs.

The crescendo is the application of research into practice. Developing meaningful communication strategies between the child with MSI, their family, peers and adults is crucial to support. Five salient strategies, combined with DIY activities and case studies, demonstrate the need for reflexive, creative and patient practitioners, capable of differentiation to accommodate various needs. The importance of background information, observation and collaboration are highlighted, guaranteeing the child is the main beneficiary. The final chapter raises poignant questions regarding responsibility, action, the requirement for further research globally, and actively responding to the bespoke needs of children with MSI. Affording children with MSI and their families space at the table stands to benefit not just the 'minority within the minority' but any child in any setting. That is inclusion, and why this book is a 'must read' for any individual concerned with MSI, disability and support.

Dr Jessica Hayton
Lecturer in Psychology
Programme Leader Graduate Diploma in Habilitation
IOE, UCL's Faculty of Education and Society, London

Preface

This book came to exist because in my fourth year of a BA in Classics, I was inspired by the film *The Sound of Silence* to learn Greek Sign Language. At some point over the course of that year, my sign language teacher, Mr Christos, asked me to teach him Spanish. At the time, I was the proud holder of a DELE Superior (Diploma de Español como Lengua Extranjera), which qualified me to teach Spanish as a foreign language. I had been offering private lessons of Ancient, Modern Greek and Latin to secondary school pupils over the course of my undergraduate studies, as an extra support for school, and had recently started to also offer Spanish lessons to a handful of adults. In my teaching practice, I had come across quite a few learners with dyslexia, hyperactivity and autistic traits, but had never taught a deaf person before.

Entering into Mr Christos' flat for the first time was like entering a completely new world. The adaptations in place to ensure everyday objects like the doorbell were accessible to him and the strategy he used to understand how to pronounce new words in Spanish, by touching my mouth and throat while I was enunciating, captivated me and made me want to know more about his world. More importantly, this experience made me think about all those learners who need adaptations to access education. This is when I decided that the next step for me would be to carry out further studies on sensory needs.

Having won a full scholarship by the Greek State for postgraduate studies abroad, I found myself in beautiful Bristol, undertaking a master's degree in special educational needs. During that academic year, which was 2003–4, I happened to come across a book by Stuart Aitken and colleagues published in 2000 about teaching deafblind children. Buying and reading this book was destined to change my life and academic trajectory for ever. If deafness had captivated me, deafblindness completely mesmerized me. I wanted to know more about it and about how I, as a teacher, could prepare myself for working with these children. I knew there and then that this was what I wanted to do, and I made it the focus of my master's dissertation.

The next milestone was writing up a research proposal in the summer of 2004, and feeling brave enough to send it to a couple of UK universities with some expertise on deafblindness. I had funding for three more years, but first needed to secure a supervisor for my doctorate! It turned out that luck was on my side, because the only person who replied to me was Dr Olga Miller at the Department of Psychology and Human Development, IOE, UCL. With her guidance, I submitted my application and I was offered a place to undertake a doctorate at this iconic institution. Moving to London in autumn 2004 was a powerful experience, but I will focus on what matters for the purposes of this preface. What matters was that Olga introduced me to another exciting world, inhabited by countless top practitioners and academics in the field, who all welcomed me to their schools, classrooms and lectures, and selflessly shared their everyday practice and wealth of experience. Among these people are friends for life, like Sue Ockelford, my Braille teacher, and Professor Adam Ockelford, as well as the numerous parents, children and young people, who welcomed me to their homes.

Reflecting on my positionality as the author of this book, I was born and trained as a teacher in Greece, but I have spent most of my adult life in England. Over the past 20 years, I have been mainly a researcher and academic focused on inclusion, disability and multisensory impairment, not a practitioner. However, this book is the result of everything that I have been taught by reading the literature, carrying out my own research, and absorbing the wisdom of experts from all over the world, whom I have been fortunate enough to meet along the way.

1 Introduction

1.1 Book focus, rationale and objectives

This book focuses on the education of children and young people with multi-sensory impairment (MSI), also known as 'deafblindness' and 'dual sensory impairment'. MSI is a combination of impairments in both distance senses (i.e. vision and hearing), which primarily affects communication, acquisition of information, independent mobility and orientation, and often co-occurs with other disabilities (Aitken 2000b). MSI is a rare and complex disability that remains underresearched (Kamenopoulou et al. 2021). More specifically, very little has been written about the participation of children and young people with MSI in education. In the current global movement towards inclusion and equal participation in education of all, it is paradoxical that very little attention has been paid to those learners with the most complex needs, for whom inclusion in education can be very challenging to achieve.

The main aim of this book is to address this gap in the literature on MSI and educational inclusion, by synthesizing theoretical literature and research evidence, and by presenting some suitable teaching strategies, alongside insights into everyday practice in the form of case studies and activities for reflection. The specific objectives of the book are to:

1 Broaden the understanding of inclusive education and argue what it may mean in the context of MSI and complex needs.
2 Raise awareness and contribute to current knowledge about an underexplored disability.
3 Provide evidence and practice-based tools, strategies and approaches that teaching professionals will find useful to know about when working with learners with MSI in any educational setting.

I first started researching MSI in 2004 as a postgraduate student for my dissertation project, which focused on teaching strategies for learners with MSI (then most commonly called 'deafblindness' in England). Since then, I have conducted research focused on children and young people with sensory impairments and complex needs, including collaborative projects with schools and universities in various countries. This book is based on almost two decades of researching and teaching about MSI and inclusive education, and has been conceived of as a much-needed resource for student teachers, teaching professionals, postgraduate researchers and academics working in the field of MSI, as well as all those interested in inclusive education for all, especially the most vulnerable. In writing this book, I wanted to engage with recent scholarship and thinking in the field, which is why I embarked on a journey to summarize and critically discuss both some of the historical and some of the current literature available, with a triple focus on research, theory and practice.

1.2 What is multisensory impairment?

1.2.1 Definition and terminology

Learners with MSI have both vision and hearing impairments of different types and degrees. These sensory impairments often coexist with other disabilities, e.g. physical disabilities or medical conditions. As I explain in the next section, MSI is extremely rare, especially in children. Additionally, one of the characteristics that children and young people with this label have in common are their differences, and this heterogeneity alongside the small size of the population with MSI worldwide could be responsible for common misconceptions and disagreements around the nature and definition of MSI, which are also reflected in the many different terms and labels still in use around the world, as well as the lack of a commonly accepted universal definition for MSI. The aim of this section is to clarify what MSI means, and at the same time to dispel some popular misconceptions about this disability.

Consider, for example, the following statements from teachers working with learners with MSI that I wrote in my field notes during a previous research project:

Teacher 1: I really like your research idea and it is fine with me to assist you with your project, but there's only one problem: Aisha does not have a multisensory impairment, she is blind and deaf.
Teacher 2: No, I don't have any students with multisensory impairments.
Me: Don't you have any students with a hearing loss in addition to their visual loss?
Teacher 2: Oh, yeah, yeah … I have loads of them!

The first common *misconception* about MSI is the assumption that it can only mean *total blindness and total deafness*. This is far from true. MSI can be either congenital, which exists from birth or early life, or acquired, which occurs later in life. Moreover, it can affect both senses at the same time or initially affect the one (e.g. hearing) and then progressively affect the other (e.g. vision). Hence it is clear that, contrary to common perceptions, the term MSI does not only refer to someone completely deaf and completely blind from birth. In terms of the time of onset of the vision and hearing impairments, MSI can take the following forms:

1 Congenital vision impairment (VI) and hearing impairment (HI)
2 Congenital VI with acquired HI
3 Congenital HI with acquired VI
4 Acquired VI and HI

Although congenital and total MSI does occur, it is nevertheless extremely rare (Miller and Hodges 2005). It is more frequently the case that both senses are impaired, but still functioning to some extent. From this, the complexity of MSI becomes clear, because its nature and impact on development can vary depending on several factors, such as the time of onset of each sensory impairment and the numerous possible combinations of hearing and vision impairments varying in kind and degree. Furthermore, the presence of additional disabilities or medical conditions, which is often the case, and the different causes, time of diagnosis and type of intervention, are all factors that complicate matters further, thus rendering it particularly difficult to include all these multifaceted aspects within a single definition. Consequently, it seems appropriate to consider each learner with MSI as a unique case that does not fit into a specific profile, which can be clearly or straightforwardly identified.

In terms of what causes MSI, congenital or early onset MSI can be caused by prematurity or complications during pregnancy and birth or a range of syndromes, the most common of which is congenital rubella syndrome, caused by a virus caught by the pregnant mother. A less common, but one of the leading causes of congenital deafblindness, is CHARGE syndrome, a complex condition characterized by a wide range of anomalies, including vision and hearing impairment (see Deuce 2017). MSI that is acquired later in life can be caused by illnesses (e.g. brain tumours), accidents (e.g. head injuries) or genetic disorders, such as Usher syndrome (see Dammeyer 2014). There are three types of Usher that vary depending on the time of onset of vision and hearing impairment – i.e. HI (severe or mild) present from birth and then progressive development of a VI (either in the first ten years in Usher type 1 or in adolescence/early adulthood in Usher type 2) and progressive development of both HI and VI after the person has learned to communicate using speech in Usher type 3. Finally, the commonest type of MSI is dual sensory loss as a result of ageing.

Indeed, there is no definition of MSI that is universally accepted and a formal and commonly accepted definition of the disability does not exist. In the England, the Department of Health adopted a working description of deafblind people as: '[p]eople whose combined sight and hearing losses cause difficulties with communication, access to information, and mobility' (DoH 1997, p. 7), which has also been incorporated in the most recent policy guidance, although instead of 'combined sight and hearing losses' the phrase 'combined sight and hearing impairment' is used (DoH 2014, p. 5).

The lack of a common definition is also reflected in the debate about the most appropriate terminology. In England, the term 'MSI' is 'usually used in relation to children and young people' (DoH 2014, p. 5), but in almost all other literature published on the topic the term 'deafblindness' is the most commonly used (Hodges et al. 2019). In this book, I mainly use the term 'MSI', since the focus is on education, but I also use the term 'deafblind' interchangeably. In relation to the latter term, however, it needs to be noted that it can be found in the literature in two forms: 'deafblindness' or 'deaf-blindness'. Regarding the difference between the two spellings, the non-hyphenated term 'deafblindness' has been argued to reflect the unique nature of the disability (Aitken 2000b), whereas the hyphenated word has been described as failing to convey that uniqueness, because it may imply that the impact of the dual sensory impairment is additive rather than multiplicative and qualitatively different from that of a single sensory impairment (SSI) (Lagatti 1995). However, some would argue that words in the English language cannot be combined in this way to create new ones and insist on using the term 'deaf-blind'. All these debates are of importance, as failing to reach an agreement on terminology and definition has implications for research, policy and practice (Kamenopoulou et al. 2021).

To sum up, MSI is *simultaneous hearing and vision impairment of any degree and nature, regardless of time of onset, intellectual ability and the presence of additional disabilities.* This definition takes into consideration the complexity of MSI, by focusing on the simultaneous presence of vision and hearing impairment, without considering the existence of other disabilities or the causes of all the above as *sine qua non* for diagnosis. The advantage of this definition is that it includes all learners with impairment in both distance senses, regardless of the time of onset, the nature and the degree of vision and hearing impairments, the causes of MSI, and the presence of additional disabilities. Even though some learners might have some useful vision or hearing, according to the above definition, they have MSI if they have impairment in both distance senses at the same time.

A final note is needed here, to clarify that the term 'MSI' is sometimes also used to describe people without hearing or vision impairment, but with sensory processing or integration issues, such as for example those experiencing extreme sensitivity to being touched or to touching certain materials, feeling sensory overload and not being able to integrate the multiple sensory inputs in visually cluttered and noisy spaces. Such issues may be experienced by people with other special educational needs/disabilities (SEN/D) such as autistic spectrum disorder (ASD) or attention deficit hyperactivity disorder (ADHD), but also the typically developing population. Children with MSI might have sensory processing or integration issues that are associated with their diagnosis (for example, being overwhelmed in visually busy environments due to the vision impairment). Other features, such as being hypersensitive or hyposensitive to sensory stimuli might not be associated with the diagnosis of MSI, but with how a particular person reacts to certain sensory experiences, as is the case in the typically developing population. Matters may become more complicated when MSI coexists with, for example, ASD in the same person, although the possibility of this scenario is still up for debate. In any case, it is a real challenge to distinguish between the features of MSI and those of ASD, because there are a lot of similarities between the two diagnoses in relation to sensory processing (but also other features, i.e. social interaction and joint attention, see Rose 2011). This book only concerns those children and young people whose development is *atypical* due to MSI, which may also be associated with sensory processing or integration issues.

1.2.2 Prevalence

It is very hard to calculate the exact number of learners with MSI due to many factors that make it difficult to identify this population. The lack of a commonly accepted definition and varied terminology in use that were discussed in the previous section are evidently significant barriers to the successful identification of individuals with MSI. Moreover, given the complexity and uniqueness of the disability, identification requires specialized resources, such as appropriate methods of assessment and professionals with prior training and experience in this particular area. Past reports that have assessed the quality of services offered to people with MSI mention this exact problem, namely, the limited availability of specialist assessment materials and the lack of trained staff responsible for carrying out these assessments (see for example, Sense 2004).

According to the first global report on the situation and rights of people with deafblindness (World Federation of the Deafblind 2018), they are a small minority group, which represents only between 0.2 to 2 per cent of the world's population. The report was based on data from one of the largest ever survey on a sample representative of the population in 22 selected countries (including low-, middle- and high-income countries), and it found differences in the definitions adopted, with some countries – for example, Ecuador, Venezuela and Iran – using the definition to describe total lack of hearing and vision, and all other countries considering deafblindness to also include some residual vision and/or hearing. More importantly, the report found that a very low percentage of people experience severe forms of deafblindness and that a higher percentage experiences milder forms, which means that severe or total deafblindness is extremely rare and mild deafblindness is more common than previously thought. Moreover, an association between age and deafblindness was found, which means that the chance of an individual becoming deafblind increases as they get older. However, the report pointed out that children and people of younger ages with deafblindness are the most affected by daily barriers – for example, in education and employment, and at the highest risk of poverty. Finally, a statistically significant gender difference was found with more women with deafblindness compared to men in most countries selected, apart from Ireland and Uruguay.

In the UK, the first most substantial survey of the population with MSI was conducted by Sense in 1988. Data-collection methods involved questionnaires sent to all counties (to health authorities, social workers, voluntary organizations and clubs for the deaf, blind and deafblind), as well as seminars to raise awareness for the survey. According to the results, there was an average of 21,000 people with MSI of all age groups in the UK (approx. 40/100,000). Survey findings ranged from 30/100,000 to 58/100,000, and according to estimates, approximately 14,000 (60 per cent) of these were elderly, thus deafblind due to ageing (Sense 1988). Nevertheless, in an article written for the Royal National Institute for the Blind (RNIB), Wadsworth (1999) suggested that based on various pieces of work undertaken nationally, this number (i.e. 40 deafblind for every 100,000 people) is an underestimate, and the same view was adopted by Sense in a subsequent report (Sense 2004). In relation to children and young people more specifically, a recent survey (Robertson and Emerson 2010) estimated 22,000 children and young people (0–19 years) in the UK have MSI. In Wales, Hodges et al. (2019) estimated about 232 children and young people (0–24 years) with MSI, based on a national estimate of 1 in 4,000 for the whole of the UK.

Another issue that prevents the collection of accurate data is the frequent overlap of the term 'MSI' with other labels used to describe learners with multiple and complex needs (for a full discussion, see Chapter 2). As mentioned before, MSI frequently co-occurs with other disabilities and medical conditions, which means that children and young people with MSI are often grouped under other labels, such as 'severe or profound and multiple learning disabilities or difficulties' (S/PMLD) or 'multiple disabilities and vision impairment' (MDVI) in the UK (and elsewhere). For example, depending on the background of the organization commissioning a survey, the terminology and its meaning may change, with clear implications for the resulting statistics. A survey by the RNIB found a prevalence rate of 2.4/1,000 blind and partially sighted children in the UK, with under 1/3 of those having additional disabilities and under 1/5 additional disabilities other than S/PMLD (Keil 2002). The same survey concluded that the proportion of deafblind children identified was under 1 per cent, but stressed that this low percentage may be precisely because of the narrow definition of deafblindness adopted in this case. In a more recent survey for the RNIB, Keil (2017) analysed statistics held by the Department for Education for the years 2016 and 2017 and found that there were 16,701 pupils with education, health and care plans (EHCPs) or on 'SEN support' with vision impairment recorded as the primary (11,592) or secondary (5,109) SEN. What is important to note here is that about half of these children had other needs apart from or in addition to vision impairment, including moderate learning difficulty (9.5 per cent), profound and multiple learning difficulty (6.9 per cent), physical disability (5.4 per cent), severe learning difficulty (4.8 per cent), and multisensory impairment (<0.5 per cent). This means that half the population of children with vision impairment have additional needs, and a small number of these have MSI. However, it is worth remembering that past reports have emphasized the high likelihood of a large number of those identified as having single sensory impairment also having unidentified dual sensory impairment (The Scottish Office 2004).

To sum up, it seems to be the case that any current figures can only be estimates, because we currently lack a reliable definition of MSI and a consistent system for counting people with MSI. Moreover, there is an urgent need for the collection and analysis of accurate data on the situation of people with deafblindness around the world. Despite those issues, based on current estimates, it nevertheless seems that MSI is a very low incidence disability and that the overall population of children and young people with MSI both in the UK and worldwide is small and extremely heterogeneous. In this sense, they can be described as a 'minority' within the minority of disabled learners.

1.3 What is inclusive education?

1.3.1 International context: the inclusion agenda and its challenges

Inclusive education is a concept created in the global North. It was first used in the late 1980s in Canada by a group of educators, writers, parents and disabled adults. In the years that followed, the concept spread quickly to the US, Canada and, afterwards, the UK. The concept continued to gain momentum and in 1994 it became part of international policy in the form of the historic Salamanca Statement and Framework for Action on Special Needs Education that was signed in Spain under the auspices of UNESCO, as a result of the World Conference on Special Needs Education. The Statement advocated for the inclusion of learners with disabilities in regular schools alongside their peers, for which reason it has come to be considered a key turning point in the history of inclusive education. Immediately after the Statement, a second wave of countries mainly in the global South began to adopt policies in relation to learners with SEN/D (see Kamenopoulou 2020).

In subsequent years, inclusive education continued to gain increasing recognition and it was specifically mentioned for the first time in a treaty document, in Article 24 of the United Nations Convention on the Rights of Persons with Disabilities (UNCRPD 2006). Recently, inclusive education has become the latest 'buzzword', always present in international agreements and gradually adopted in national policies of countries across the North and South (Slee 2018). The sustainable development goals (SDGs) adopted by the United Nations in September 2015 reinforced this, with SDG4, the global goal for education, calling on countries to 'ensure inclusive and equitable quality education and promote lifelong learning opportunities for all' by 2030. This was followed by the Incheon Declaration and Framework for the Implementation of SDG4, adopted after the World Education Forum held in the Republic of Korea in May 2015. A recent global education monitoring report (GEM) (UNESCO 2020) was the first of its kind to explore worldwide progress towards inclusive education, focusing on learners who are disadvantaged and at risk for exclusion from education.

Although the rhetoric of inclusive education has undoubtedly spread across the globe, evidence shows that when implemented in practice, a plethora of challenges remain across all countries. Examples include context- or country-specific issues, such as the lack of infrastructure and funding for inclusive education in global South countries, where local realities are very different from the wealthier education systems of the global North, from which inclusive education initially emerged. Other challenges however can be described as universal, since they are faced by both countries of the North and South, such as the lack of appropriate teacher training for implementing inclusive education in practice. For more about the distinction between context-specific and universal barriers to inclusive education, see Kamenopoulou (2018). What is relevant to note here is that possibly the biggest universal challenge is the lack of a clear definition of 'inclusive education', which results in very different understandings of what it actually means across local contexts and has significant implications for policy and practice. There is lack of agreement as to who the focus of inclusion should be: is it those children with SEN/D, the wider group of children vulnerable to exclusion or all children? (see Cigman 2007; Kiuppis 2014). Since the Salamanca Statement placed emphasis on the right of children with SEN/D to be educated in mainstream schools alongside their peers, an idea that was revolutionary at the time, one of the most popular understandings of inclusion has come to be as 'locational inclusion' or 'placement of children with SEN/D in mainstream schools'. Proponents of this understanding are concerned with where children are placed, and they emphasize that children with SEN/D have the right to be in mainstream schools, and that segregated provision is the complete opposite of a just education system (see for example, Slee 2019).

Two questions are relevant to ask here: 1) Does this view fail to consider if mainstream placement would indeed constitute *inclusive and equitable quality education* for all learners, including those with complex needs? and 2) Should placement be the main focus? At the same time that the dominant discourse conceptualizing inclusive education as a 'place' is steadily spreading across countries of the North and South, a number of leading authors (see for example, in England, Warnock 2005; Hornby 2015; Hodkinson 2019) emphasize that the focus should not be on placement but on the quality of provision, since mere mainstream placement does not ensure inclusion and participation. In light of this, one might correctly point out that the international movement for inclusive education tends to be too heavily (and unhelpfully) focused on placement, i.e. where children should be educated, instead of being concerned with the quality of education they receive in any educational setting, where they are placed. This is the principle upon which this book is based, i.e. the idea that the quality of the education that a child with MSI receives is much more important than the type of placement. Hence for the sake of clarity, this book adopts the following definition: 'inclusive education concerns the participation in education of all children and especially of the most vulnerable ones, i.e. those who have traditionally been either excluded or at risk for exclusion from the education system' (Kamenopoulou 2018: 2). This definition covers all children, but places emphasis on the most vulnerable, including those with disabilities. More importantly, this definition does not specify where children should be placed and does not consider mainstream placement as a necessary prerequisite for inclusion, since the focus is on children's participation in education regardless of setting.

In relation to the inclusion and participation in education of children with complex needs, like those with MSI, two current issues can be identified. The first issue is the number of children, who are at the high end of the spectrum of ability and therefore can be in mainstream schools, following the same curriculum as other children with the right adaptations and support, but are excluded and placed in segregated settings, not because of their disabilities, but because the mainstream school system cannot meet their needs or because it is wrongly thought that they cannot cope in a mainstream setting. Research on vision impairment for example, has found parents to value special schools for many reasons, including availability of specialized resources and staff, which mainstream schools do not always have (Miller et al. 2008). Moreover, the choice parents make about placement depends on their perceptions of their child's abilities and disabilities, and it is also influenced by cultural beliefs and expectations about what disabled people can achieve (Chu and Lo 2016). Additionally, parents of typically developing children have been reported to hold negative views about the placement of children with complex needs in mainstream classrooms (de Boer and Munde 2015). Last but not least, research on teaching professionals and policymakers has also shown negative attitudes towards the placement of children with complex needs in mainstream schools. It has been found that they consider mainstream school placement appropriate or achievable only for some children but not for others, depending on the type and severity of SEN, and that those learners with profound, multiple and complex needs are seen as the most difficult to include. This has been supported by studies in both Northern contexts (see for example, Croll and Moses 2000; Avramidis and Norwich 2002; Evans and Lunt 2002) and Southern contexts (see for example, Kartika and Kuroda 2019).

The second issue that can be identified concerns those children at the low end of the spectrum of ability who would benefit from special school placement. Access to special schools with the right resources and professional expertise is not always available as a local option. The real problem here is the lack of funding, resources and specialized support. For example, in my research in a range of different contexts – including, Colombia, Romania, Greece and Cyprus – I have met children and young people who have to travel very long distances to reach the special school they attend and, in many cases, have to attend residential provision. Moreover, statistics show that in many countries high numbers of children and young people with complex needs remain out of school. In many global South contexts, such as for example, in Colombia, those children and young people with complex needs are excluded from an education system that is not yet able to include them, and instead attend institutions of a non-educational nature run by the social services that focus on vocational and life skills (Kamenopoulou 2020). In some countries, such as for example India, there is a specific law about the right of children with complex disabilities to opt for home schooling (UNESCO 2019). The GEM report (UNESCO 2020) provides further snippets of information on the current situation of children with complex disabilities worldwide, such as for example that there is evidence of a high percentage of drop outs as children with complex needs progress through the education system, especially in poorer countries. Finally, the first global report on deafblindness (World Federation of the Deafblind 2018) found that children with MSI are 17 times less likely to be in school than typically developing children.

1.3.2 The argument: Why is this book necessary?

As Imray and Colley (2017) point out, the extensive literature on inclusive education has rarely considered what form(s) inclusion might take in reality for learners with the most complex needs, hence it is safe to argue that debates around inclusive education have so far failed to consider these groups, and what inclusion in education might look like for them in practice. Furthermore, recent research shows that mechanisms developed to safeguard the implementation of UNCRPD have not been successful in capturing the perspectives and experiences of those learners with the most complex needs (Byrne 2019). A review of research on MSI in education found that the children's and young people's perspectives and experiences are rarely explored (Kamenopoulou et al. 2021). This suggests that those most at risk for marginalization and exclusion are at the same time the least likely to have a voice in debates pertaining to their right to quality education. It follows from these points that the various 'experts' need to pay more attention to how inclusive education is experienced or not by those vulnerable children and young people in practice, and what *quality educational provision* might mean for this particular group of learners.

In relation to the latter, one of the biggest barriers to quality provision is the lack of enough or adequate teacher training and preparation for inclusive education that has been consistently reported in relation to both Northern and Southern contexts (as mentioned in the previous section, and as discussed in detail in Kamenopoulou et al. 2016; see also, Kamenopoulou 2018). This is an unexplained gap, given that in addition to its most well-known aspect (i.e. stipulating that children with disabilities should be educated in regular schools alongside their peers), the 1994 Salamanca Statement furthermore acknowledged the preparation of all educational personnel as a key factor contributing to the success of inclusive education and also provided guidelines on teacher preparation. Yet more than 25 years after Salamanca, teacher preparation for inclusive education remains patchy at universal level and an area in need of urgent development across countries of the North and South.

The lack of teacher training and preparation for inclusive education can hamper inclusion in two ways. First, research has shown that teacher training on inclusive education can reverse negative attitudes, with those teachers who receive training developing positive attitudes. For example, Boyle et al. (2013) found that even by studying a single postgraduate module on special education can lead to positive attitudes towards inclusion. Crucially, this has been shown to be the case for both pre-service and in-service training. Sahamkhadam (2020) conducted a systematic review of intervention studies targeting in-service teachers in mainstream schools and the findings supported the effectiveness of interventions to promote positive attitudes towards inclusion in teachers. Lautenbach and Heyder (2019) conducted a systematic review of training programmes aimed at pre-service teachers and found that such programmes can lead to change in teachers' attitudes.

The second way, in which lack of teacher training hampers inclusion, concerns more specifically the needs of some learners. It needs to be pointed out that the debate around what teacher preparation for inclusive education should include is ongoing, with some arguing that there is no need for teachers to use special pedagogies to address the needs of special learners, because all learners benefit from the same continuum of inclusive approaches (Norwich and Lewis 2007), and others criticizing this approach arguing that special education knowledge is a crucial component of teacher training (Mintz and Wyse 2015). The latter authors point to research showing that lack of knowledge about specific groups of learners hampers teachers' ability to implement inclusive approaches and address diverse needs (see Kamenopoulou et al. 2016). Article 24 of the UNCRPD, which specifically mentions deafblindness, calls on states to ensure that the education of children with single or dual sensory impairment is delivered in the most appropriate *means of communication*, and in educational environments that support their academic achievement and social development. On the basis of this, it can be argued that when teachers are not equipped with specialized strategies that are suitable for working with specific learners, such as for example knowledge of Braille, when working with learners who are blind/visually impaired, this hampers their ability to implement inclusion.

Currently in the UK there is only one training programme for teachers, which leads to a nationally recognized qualification on MSI, offered by the University of Birmingham. Specialized knowledge about MSI remains the expertise of some special schools with a long history of meeting the needs of learners with MSI, such as the MSI Unit at the Victoria School in Birmingham and the Whitefield Academy Trust in London, which have developed their own initiatives, including bespoke personalized curricula, policies for identification, assessment of and provision for learners with MSI, and staff training (see Chapter 4). In my own research, I have seen a similar pattern in many different countries, including Bhutan, Colombia, Cyprus, Greece and Romania, where appropriate strategies, educational programmes and interventions for MSI developed by specialized schools are not systematized or disseminated outside of these settings. The first report on the situation of people with MSI around the world (World Federation of the Deafblind 2018) confirms that, in the international landscape, there are very limited and inconsistent opportunities for teachers to gain specialized knowledge on MSI.

To sum up, the main argument of this book is that in order to be able to meet our global target of including all children in education, we desperately need more resources that support professionals working with those children with complex needs, such as those with MSI, who have thus far been overlooked by the breadth of research and theoretical literature on inclusive education and SEN/D. I decided to write this book because ignoring the learners, who might challenge us the most, is quite simply no longer an option. Now that inclusive education is readily accepted as the right approach morally and increasingly adopted by countries around the world, it is appropriate to also turn our attention to those learners, whose inclusion in education is bound to be challenging and to consider what form inclusive education might take for those learners in practice. I argue that by focusing on the most vulnerable, we will better prepare future teachers to make inclusion in education for all a reality and not a utopia.

1.4 Overview of chapters

Chapter 2 is divided into two sections, and its aim is to establish what we know so far about MSI, based on a chronological, geographical and thematic review of the limited, but important, research literature on MSI and education. The first section provides a brief historical overview of early pioneering work in the US and the Soviet Union, and then I move on to present some of the work carried out in the late twentieth century, mainly in the US, the Netherlands and the UK. In the second section of Chapter 2, I provide a review of research studies carried out in the last 20 years on the topic of MSI and education, with a special focus on England as a case study, but also on some other countries. At the end of Chapter 2, I provide some reflections on future directions for research on MSI.

In Chapter 3, I draw on theoretical literature to discuss the impact of MSI on child development with reference to primary and secondary difficulties faced by the individual, and I finish the chapter by considering the implications that MSI could have for learning and participation in education. Chapter 4 is focused on best practices, and it is the longest chapter of the book, because it includes vignettes, case studies, tools, independent activities and further readings. These resources are designed to help professionals make their teaching more inclusive of learners with MSI, and they will also be useful to lecturers teaching about MSI and complex needs, as well as researchers working in this field. I begin this chapter by discussing the main areas of need of children with MSI in education, and in the second and main part of the chapter I present and critically discuss appropriate strategies and approaches for supporting children with MSI in education. I conclude the chapter with some key recommendations for practitioners.

In Chapter 5, which is the final chapter, I reiterate the main argument of the book – i.e. that in the context of the current global trend towards inclusion of all learners in education, we must also focus on supporting those learners with complex needs, for whom inclusion can admittedly be very challenging to achieve, including those with MSI. I draw on all chapters to provide reflections on the key messages emerging from this book and to discuss some of the exciting possibilities that lie ahead for future research, theory and practice in the field of MSI. In the Appendix, I provide a list of relevant websites with useful information and resources, and at the end of the book, there is a detailed Index with all key names and terms mentioned in the chapters.

2 Research: review of the literature

2.1 Cautionary note on reviewing the literature on MSI

Many years of conducting research in this field have taught me that thoroughly reviewing the scarce research literature on MSI can be a daunting task, for many reasons. Firstly, as I explained in Chapter 1, various terms are being used in different countries or even within the same country by different authors to describe MSI and also, historically, different terms have been adopted. As a result, identifying relevant studies will require multiple database searches with the use of several 'keywords', including, but not limited to, 'MSI', 'deafblindness', and 'dual sensory impairment'. As an illustrative example of how the term often changes depending on the author(s), the era, and the geographical context, it is worth mentioning that Bakhurst and Padden (1991) use the term 'blind-deaf' when writing about the seminal work of Alexander Meshcheryakov in the Soviet Union, although in the English translation of his book, the term 'deaf-blind' is used throughout (Meshcheryakov 1979).

Secondly, as I explain in detail in this chapter, nowadays many other terms are used to describe or categorize children with complex needs, and children with MSI might fall under these categories. As an example, in the UK context, some of the most commonly used terms to describe complex needs are: in England, severe learning disabilities or difficulties (SLD), profound and multiple learning disabilities or difficulties (PMLD), multiple disabilities (MD) or multiple disabilities and vision impairment (MDVI); in Scotland, complex learning difficulties and disabilities (CLDD). As a result of this, when trying to identify literature that might be relevant or applicable to learners with MSI, one needs to bear in mind that those with MSI can be one type or group of learners who fall under these generic and thus far poorly defined categories (Ockelford 2008; Kamenopoulou et al. 2021). It is therefore helpful to emphasize that in most cases, regardless of the label being used, reviewing the relevant research will require a careful examination of:

1. How the researchers define the population that is the focus of their study.
2. How they describe the characteristics of their specific sample/research participants.

This brings me to the third reason why it is difficult to conduct a holistic and comprehensive review of the literature on learners with MSI or of the literature, which might be applicable to those learners, namely, the great variation in how different studies are reported when published. As I will highlight in the second section of this chapter, which reviews research conducted in the twenty-first century, many articles published in peer-reviewed academic journals, rather surprisingly given the lack of commonly accepted definitions for the terms used, do not include transparent information regarding the focus population or the characteristics of the specific research participants thus making it hard to establish if the study concerns learners with MSI or learners with other complex needs without the presence of vision and hearing impairments. As a result, when reporting the findings, studies tend to lump together children with complex needs, without differentiating the results that may relate to children with MSI as a distinct group. This may result in biased claims (e.g. that an intervention is effective for children with PMLD or complex needs, without demonstrating its effectiveness for different groups, such as those with MSI). This is why it is important to always conduct a detailed analysis of the research study in question, including the sample characteristics and the description of the population.

Notwithstanding these limitations, in this chapter I aim to establish what we know so far, based on a chronological, geographical and thematic review of the limited, but important, research literature on MSI and education. I begin with a historical overview of early pioneering work in the US and the then Soviet Union, and after that I move on to a discussion of the research from the late twentieth century, focusing on the US, the Netherlands and the UK. Following this, I present a scoping review of research studies conducted in the last 20 years on the topic of MSI and inclusion in education, focusing both on England as a case study, and internationally. In the final section of the chapter I identify gaps in our current knowledge and indicate areas in which more research is urgently needed. Throughout this section, I have maintained the terminology used by the author(s), while for overlapping labels I specify whether MSI was included in the sample or if this information was unspecified by the authors.

2.2 Brief historical overview

2.2.1 Early pioneering work in the US

In popular culture, the most well-known educator in the history of deafblindness is Anne Sullivan, the teacher of Helen Keller (born in 1880 in the US), who became famous for her achievements 'despite' the fact that she had become deafblind at an early age, because she lived at a time when 'the general orthodoxy suggested that there was limited, if any, potential for those considered to be deafblind' (Miller and Hodges 2005: 43). Before Helen Keller, Laura Bridgman, who was born in 1829, is recorded as the first deafblind person to be educated in the US. She was taught by Samuel Howe, who was a medical doctor and the first director of Perkins School for the Blind (McLetchie 1995). His approach focused on teaching Laura symbolic communication by helping her match labels in raised print to objects, and he also taught her fingerspelling.

Table 2.1 Early pioneering work in the US: key learning points

• Perkins School for the Blind in the US is a school and centre providing services to children with MSI and training on MSI for teachers. • Laura Bridgman and Helen Keller are two of the most well-known deafblind people in history, and both were educated at Perkins. • Anne Sullivan, Helen's teacher, based her teaching approach on the writings of Samuel Howe, the director of Perkins, who had taught Laura before, and her approach would today be considered 'best practice'.

Before Helen Keller joined Perkins, Anne Sullivan, who had recently graduated from the same school, consulted Howe's writings to prepare for teaching Helen. She first established communication and rapport with the student by fingerspelling into her hands, and then she helped her make the connection between the word being spelled and what it represents (famously, the first word she learned to associate with what it symbolizes was 'water'). After this initial connection was made, 'Helen's progress was rapid in receptive and expressive language. Teaching occurred in natural environments that were meaningful and age appropriate. Vocabulary was determined by the child's interests and motivation. Anne Sullivan's methods would today be considered best practices' (McLetchie 1995: 92). Perkins School for the Blind in Massachusetts is today one of the word-leading schools specializing in the education of children with vision impairment and additional disabilities, including MSI, and it also provides teacher training courses, webinars and a range of other online resources.

2.2.2 Early pioneering work in the Soviet Union

I always advise students interested in MSI to start by reading the book of Soviet psychologist Alexander Meshcheryakov: *Awakening to Life* (1979). This pioneering book systematically describes the educational work conducted with pupils with profound MSI at the Institute for Research into Physical and Mental Handicaps between 1955 and 1970, and at the home for deafblind children in Zagorsk, Russia, between 1963 and 1970. Meshcheryakov completed this book in 1974, and it was translated and published in English in 1979, five years after his death at the age of 51. Meshcheryakov saw the teaching of deafblind children like an interdisciplinary experiment in the fields of psychology and special needs education. He adopted a systematic approach in both his teaching and his research and put together detailed descriptions of the developmental trajectory of unique cases of children in the form of case studies.

Meshcheryakov's theory focused on those children who were congenitally deafblind, although he also had students with MSI acquired later in life, and as a result, his writings are 'essentially a "worse case scenario" embodying a general educative framework which he believed applicable to less severe cases' (Bakhurst and Padden 1991: 203). The main aim of his approach was to foster independence in children, who were in the first instance totally dependent on others for accessing and experiencing the world. Accordingly, the teacher's role was to help the child first establish an idea of self, by acquiring an understanding of others. One of the key methods teachers used at the Zagorsk home for deafblind children was *modelling*. With vision and hearing, two major channels of information not fully functioning or totally missing, experience of the world and its elements, including people and objects, can be limited. This means that the usual strategies automatically employed by most people for acquiring information about their surrounding world, such as *observation* and *imitation*, are barely included in these children's repertoire. Children with profound MSI have a limited ability for *incidental learning*, i.e. they do not automatically learn by experience or by observing and imitating others. As a result, in order for cognitive development to occur, the external world and all its elements, for example, people and objects, must be deliberately introduced by the teacher. However, Meshcheryakov demonstrated that this is not a one-way process with the child being a passive receptor of input from the outside world. The process will equally depend on the child's developmental level and it will initially be built around the satisfaction of the child's basic needs with the acquisition of self-care skills. Hence close *observation* of a particular child also emerges as necessary, because it is only through a holistic knowledge of a child's unique potential that one can establish communication and rapport, crucial for social interaction to take place. More importantly, it is the assimilation of this social experience that helps the child develop cognitively, according to Meshcheryakov.

The influence of Soviet psychologist Lev Vygotsky is clear on the theoretical framework that shaped Meshcheryakov's thinking about deafblindness and the development of the human mind. Despite the numerous translations and interpretations of the writings of Vygotsky in the different editions of his books over the years, three general conclusions can be drawn about the central themes of Vygotsky's theoretical framework: 1) the perception of development *as not a product but a process*, 2) the notion that this process occurs during *social interactions*, and 3) the focus on the need to understand the *tools* mediating this process (Wertsch 1985). According to this framework, cognitive development takes place as a result of social interaction, because all higher mental functions are internalized social relationships (Vygotsky 1978). During the process of internalization, the role of communication systems is considered vital, because they are the tools through which social interaction takes place and, consequently, they underpin cognitive development. Vygotsky argued that barriers to participation in social interchange can impact on cognitive development and that such barriers can be both biological and social (Daniels 2001).

The Vygotskian framework stressed the role of the adult during interactions, because they act as the *mediator* between child and social context. It moreover highlighted the role that atypical biological characteristics can play in these interactions, with obvious implications for the development of children with profound deafblindness. Accordingly, Meshcheryakov argued for the role of *joint activity* in cognitive development. Hence the key idea behind his work is that the deafblind child must be made aware of its self and its needs, and taught to independently satisfy these needs. But in order to foster awareness of self, the teacher has to make the child aware of the external world. The teacher needs to bring the external world into the mind of the child, by working on the basis of a particular child's existing potential for communication and interaction. Vygotsky's 'zone of proximal development' (ZPD) underpins this process: close observation of the child allows a thorough knowledge of his/her abilities and needs, and helps the teacher regulate the amount and type of support needed for the child to be able to complete the activity independently. Hence any attempt to teach children with MSI must be tailored to their level of development. It is also relevant to note here, that the concept of *scaffolding*, introduced by Bruner (1990) to describe the support provided by the adult when the child is learning a new skill or completing a new task, is closely related to that of ZPD, and that the two terms are often used interchangeably in both theory and practice.

Marxist philosophy also emerges as extremely influential in Meshcheryakov's thinking about how the human mind develops. Indeed, he described his work as evidence supporting Marx's theoretical view of development as assimilation of social experience. Prior to Meshcheryakov, many prominent psychologists had adopted Marx's theoretical work and argued that it is the interaction between individual and context that underpins cognitive development. Lev Vygotsky and Alexei Leontiev were pioneers of this wave of thought and were the founders of the 'sociohistorical school of Soviet Psychology' (Bakhurst and Padden 1991: 202). Renowned philosophers like Evald Ilyenkov also adopted the same theoretical perspective and considered thought as immanent to existence – in other words, playing an active role in development. Ilyenkov's relationship with Meshcheryakov is described in Bakhurst's book: *Consciousness and Revolution in Soviet Philosophy* (1991). Similarly, Meshcheryakov based his practical and theoretical work with profoundly deafblind children on the principle that the human mind is the product of interaction between the individual and others in an environment created by human labour. He undertook the task of shaping human behaviour and cognition in profoundly deafblind children by working on the basis of the humanizing influence of objects created by society. He maintained that it is through interaction with these objects that the child can internalize and understand their social meaning.

A final important point that we can take away from Meshcheryakov's pioneering book is the intriguing rationale that he provided in support of the need to study deafblindness. He pointed out that studying the cognitive development of deafblind children is a vital source of information for the role that vision and hearing play in typical development and for the way the human mind develops in general. Because children who are profoundly deafblind cannot readily have access to information available in the social world that surrounds them, on the basis of his work, he argues that it is crucial to observe these children in order to understand the role of *external input* in how the human mind and consciousness develop. This rationale was eloquently captured by Leontiev (1948: 108): 'Deaf-blindness is the most extreme experiment on man, an experiment devised by Nature herself, and one of the most complex and awe-inspiring phenomena

Table 2.2 Early pioneering work in the Soviet Union: Meshcheryakov key learning points

- Theoretical framework: view of development as assimilation of social experience – influenced by ideas of Vygotsky, Leontiev, Ilyenkov and Marx.
- Teaching approach: teacher deliberately introduces elements of the external world, establishes joint activity, closely observes child's potential and needs, models use of objects, and progressively fosters child's independence – relates to concepts of ZPD (Vygotsky 1978) and scaffolding (Bruner 1990).
- Research on MSI: understanding of how external sensory input (vision and hearing) shapes typical brain development, exploration of the development of human mind and behaviour.

– the inner mechanism of the emergent human consciousness in the objective relationships which mould that consciousness.' On a different level, Meshcheryakov's work provided strong evidence for the relevance and value of qualitative observational methods of enquiry in psychology and disability studies, in their quest of understanding human development. With his detailed case studies of children with unique characteristics, Meshcheryakov was able to provide valid and reliable answers to universal philosophical questions around the birth and development of human mind and behaviour.

2.2.3 The late twentieth century: work in the Netherlands, UK and US

A lot of published research on MSI in the late twentieth century was done in the US and the UK, and here I focus on these two countries. Research from that period can be found in academic publications, but a large part has been published in grey literature (which is also included here where relevant), but also in books aimed at practitioners that have had a huge impact on the field, and I refer to these books throughout Chapter 4 that explores practical strategies for including children with MSI in education. It is necessary to note here that the work of Jan van Dijk in the Netherlands from that period has been extremely influential in the field of deafblindness. Van Dijk was a leading expert in the field of deafblindness, who traced his expertise in the rubella epidemic in Europe and the US in the 1960s (Miller and Hodges 2005). Like Meshcheryakov, his work was influenced by Vygotsky's ideas about the role that the social and cultural context plays in development, but it also draws on the theories of Piaget and Bowlby. As a result of his pioneering work with deafblind children, he developed the concepts of *resonance, attachment, co-active movement,* and *natural communication.* I discuss the theoretical underpinnings of van Dijk's work further in Chapter 3 and the influential pedagogical approach that he developed in Chapter 4.

Sense in the UK first began as a charity supporting deafblind people, but over the years its work expanded and now they support a wide range of people with complex communication needs (including MSI). As mentioned in Chapter 1, in 1988 Sense conducted the first substantial survey of the deafblind population in the UK. Apart from estimating the prevalence of deafblindness in the country, the survey also looked at school placement of children and young people with MSI, and found that at the time segregation in special schools was the norm, which might be one reason why there are few, if any, studies within mainstream schools from the UK in this period. The report recommended the design and implementation of new studies in what was then (and to a great extent still is to this day) a groundbreaking field. Another survey of local education authorities (LEAs) and specialist schools by Sense focused on the range of services available for children with MSI in England and Wales at the time (Boothroyd 1997). The survey found that specialized services were starting to be developed and that the number of teachers with specialist MSI training was starting to rise. Moreover, the vast majority of children with MSI both at primary and secondary school levels were placed in schools for children with SLD and there was an increase in children with MSI, who had additional disabilities and/or medical conditions. Assessment was identified by the survey as an area that lacked strategic planning in many participating LEAs.

Research on the *assessment* of children with vision impairment and multiple needs, emphasized the importance of having accurate information about vision for education purposes, because it helps guide decisions when setting targets. Having accurate information about functional vision, including near and distance vision when working with a learner with vision impairment, also helps the teacher focus on what the child can actually do with their usable vision, instead of treating them as blind (Dunnett 1990). Moreover, in the case of vision impairment and multiple disabilities, others stressed the role of flexible assessment methods that capture the impact of individual disabilities but also their compounding effects, the role of multidisciplinary work, and a strong collaboration with parents (Laffan 1997).

Porter et al. (1997) conducted research on the *teaching strategies* that teachers in England used to ensure *curriculum access* for deafblind children in mainstream and special settings. In total, 57 teachers and 82 pupils took part in the study, which involved questionnaires and teacher logs, and a total of 145 strategies were identified. I refer to their findings that concern teaching strategies in Chapter 4. In relation to the differences between settings, they found that deafblind pupils in mainstream schools were often taught the national curriculum with support (e.g. Braille, signing sessions) rather than modified or developmental curricula and that teachers in mainstream schools mainly focused on making the curriculum accessible, such as considering the pupil's physical position in relation to sound. Moreover, children, who were taught the national curriculum, received 25 per cent of one-to-one tuition compared to 59 per cent of children taught developmental and 55 per cent of children taught modified curricula.

During this same period, researchers in England also focus systematically on *communication development* in learners with vision impairment and complex needs, such as for example interventions for supporting learners progress from the use of concrete symbols (objects of reference, see Ockelford and Park 2002) to an abstract tactile code (such as Moon, see McLinden 1995) and raised symbolic communication systems (see Hendrickson and McLinden 1995). McLinden (1999) then continued focusing on haptic exploratory strategies used by children with vision impairment and additional disabilities, including hearing impairment, and on the development of interventions for quantitatively and qualitatively improving the processing of information perceived through the sense of touch. In Chapter 4, I discuss these strategies in more detail. I review the work that McLinden and colleagues from the University of Birmingham then went on to conduct in this area in section 2.3.

One of the ways in which research from the US differs from that conducted in the UK, is that the former has explored mainstream settings much more. Within this body of work, one of the topics that has been looked at in more depth, compared to the UK context, is the *social participation* of learners with MSI in mainstream schools, and I will focus on this topic here. It needs to be noted that this body of work is still relatively limited, but at the same time its small size allows a thorough scrutiny and critical discussion of relevant studies. Like other groups of disabled children, the literature suggests that social inclusion is a complex issue for learners with MSI, influenced by both individual and contextual factors. When presenting research from the US in the rest of this section, I first discuss exploratory studies, then interventions, and lastly, I consider research related to the topic of social inclusion in a broader way.

Exploratory studies on children and young people with MSI in mainstream schools indicate an increased amount of peer interaction in these settings, but, contrary to other studies on disabled children that report positive outcomes for both interactions and relationships, research on MSI raises serious concerns as to the extent to which increased peer interaction that occurs in mainstream settings can lead to stable friendship networks. Romer and Haring (1994) looked at the social participation of students with deafblindness to explore the extent to which they were included in their schools and how this inclusion influenced their social interactions and contacts with non-disabled peers. The 12 participants varied greatly in terms of age, type and cause of deafblindness. Moreover, apart from one student, who was fully enrolled in the local mainstream school, the rest of the participants were in a special education classroom and shared time with their non-disabled peers during certain parts of the school day. The main method of data collection was the completion of cards by teachers providing information on activities, in which the children with deafblindness engaged with peers. Information included description and duration of the activity, the name of the peer joining the student in the activity and the place where interaction occurred. Data were gathered over a period of one year and six months with the teachers completing the cards on a weekly basis, but focusing on a single day, which rotated each week. According to the results, the deafblind students experienced a significant amount of contact with increased numbers of same age peers when in mainstream education environments. However, they also found that students with more time spent with peers had not developed a stable network of peer contacts, but tended to experience interactions with different peers each time. They concluded that opportunities for peer interaction provided in mainstream education environments may be increased, but not influential enough to foster long-lasting relationships. The authors acknowledged that their data was predominantly quantitative and therefore a different research design would have allowed further exploration of the nature of peer relationships. Accordingly, simply measuring the amount of time spent with peers is an insufficient indicator of inclusion and participation, in the sense that it does not capture information on the nature of the relationships established between the interacting students. Furthermore, the main sources of data in this study were the teachers; the views of the students would have been useful, especially in relation to evaluating the quality of the relationships developed during time spent together. Finally, the authors stressed that if a common system of communication does not exist between the child with MSI and their peers, it is difficult for them to establish a relationship, and accordingly, they maintained that this might constitute a major setback in the social lives of deafblind students, regardless of educational setting.

Mar and Sall (1995) implemented and evaluated an *intervention* programme to enhance opportunities for deafblind students to participate in activities with mainstream peers. In line with Romer and Haring (1994), the three participants varied in terms of type and degree of deafblindness, and educational placement, as two were in self-contained special classrooms and one in a regular classroom. Again, adults were the source of data, but in this study the parents of the students were also involved in the implementation of the intervention and the collection of data. Data-collection methods included questionnaires and checklists administered to the teachers and parents before and after the intervention. Data collected was twofold: teachers and parents reported the frequency of opportunities for spending time engaged in activities with peers, as well as the frequency of their actual occurrence in both school and community. Moreover, a social network analysis was carried out with respect to the deafblind students' most frequent and closest interactive partners. Results showed that interventions involving school, home and community may increase the amount of opportunities for social participation. However, consistent with Romer and Haring, it was also found that despite the increase of time spent in activities with peers, the number of friendship networks remained very *low* and the majority had a *transient* nature. The authors therefore called for more research to illuminate the nature of peer relationships of deafblind children, as well as the nature of difficulties that seem to influence the development of friendships. However, they argued that mainstream schools provide increased opportunities for social participation compared with special schools.

Other *intervention studies* designed to increase social participation of children and young people with MSI from the same period seem to consistently report positive results. Haring et al. (1995) explored the possibility of applying a peer support intervention with a view to enhance social networks and relationships in mainstream settings. The networks included one or two initial close peers, who were chosen on the basis of the common interests they shared with the deafblind student and were asked to spend time with him/her and to include him/her in their ordinary activities, for example during breaktime. The peers offering support were also asked to collaborate with each other and share thoughts about how to best include the deafblind students in their activities. Positive results were reported, including increased peer interaction, greater accessibility of activities and durable friendship networks. It could therefore be concluded from this study that interventions might be more effective if they are focused on the establishment of peer networks rather than dyadic relationships.

Along the same lines, but primarily focusing on enhancing communication rather than creating a supportive social context, DeCaluwe et al. (1999) developed an intervention in order to familiarize the peers with aspects of deafblindness in general, as well as with the personal profile of a specific deafblind student. The communication portfolio (CP) aims to develop the communication partner's competence by providing a wide range of information about the deafblind pupil's unique needs, abilities and preferences. Photographs, texts, videos and other materials are included in the CPs in order to provide a holistic view to all possible interacting partners. The researchers argued that access to person-specific information supports peers in understanding how to appropriately approach the deafblind student and make interaction a rewarding experience for everyone involved. The central role of the family members in providing information about the child was stressed, which calls for active family involvement in deafblind children's education.

Finally, indirect ways of improving social inclusion have been suggested, such as the creation of conditions that naturally motivate children to participate in reciprocal interactions and to develop mutual relationships. The aim here is to organize leisure time activities of a creative and recreational nature, that are argued to be enjoyable and thus, appealing to all students (Welch and Goetz 1997). Interactive story making (Miles 2000) is a technique designed to facilitate deafblind students' participation in literacy, which is argued to offer increased opportunities for peer interaction and the development of social skills. Moreover, playing has also been argued to be central to the development of deafblind children (see for example, Moss 1995). The contribution of recreational and physical activities in reducing deafblind individuals' social isolation and in meeting their physical, emotional and social needs has also been explored (Lieberman 2002). Lieberman and Taule (1997) argued that those activities are beneficial for deafblind children not only physically, since they develop body awareness for example, but also socially and psychologically, as it has been observed that they may help reduce challenging behaviour and increase peer interaction. However, it should be acknowledged that including deafblind children in physical activities can be difficult due to limitations related to mobility, orientation and the need to use their hands for many of these activities.

Studies from the US exploring other topics also provide some useful data on the social interactions and relationships of pupils with MSI in mainstream schools. Giangreco et al. (1991) explored parental perspectives using qualitative interviews. Among the themes that emerged, the most relevant were: a) that the lack of social networks of a stable nature constituted one of the parents' primary concerns, because most social contacts experienced by their children during leisure time were with family members or with friends of family members, and b) that concerning educational placement parents were not against mainstreaming, but against change of setting, which suggests that they valued a stable school environment more than a specific type of placement (mainstream or special). The authors underlined that it is important for teachers to respect and value parents' views, but also pointed out some common challenges in the collaboration between family and school such as the fact that parents did not always feel satisfied with their level of participation in decisions affecting their child's education.

Following a literature review, Downing and Eichinger (1990) concluded that appropriate adaptations and modifications are prerequisites for successful mainstream placement. They presented and critically analysed the various strategies available to make the school accessible to deafblind students both academically and socially. In terms of ensuring positive social participation, they stressed the peers' role in modelling appropriate social skills and they maintained that withdrawal for one-to-one teaching sessions impedes socialization and independence, because the child merely acquires and practises the social skills required in adult-directed interactions, skills that are not always applicable or transferable to peer interactions. They therefore suggested the adoption of alternative strategies for teaching deafblind children in mainstream schools, such as small group instruction and cooperative learning, both of which offer opportunities for the children to learn while taking part in peer group activities.

In a quite different study on the development of partner-friendly communication systems, Heller et al. (1995) argued that in order to maximize peer acceptance, greater visibility of deafblind people is needed in both school and community, because this raises the peers' awareness of aspects of the disability, such as its implications for communication. Adopting a similar rationale, Huebner et al. (1995) explored the role of the teachers and the use of an in-service training manual. The target group comprised teachers without prior experience in teaching deafblind students and the results showed a rise in self-confidence and development of positive attitudes towards teaching deafblind students post-intervention. Welch and Goetz (1997) report on the findings of a group of professionals working with deafblind young people that was formed with a view to evaluate the inclusiveness of educational placements across the US. The group conducted several case studies and among the issues identified were the need for ongoing teacher training, integrated services and parental involvement. Moreover, the need to develop the students' sense of belonging in the school's life emerged as a necessary component of an effective inclusive programme.

To summarize, research from the US that has explored different aspects of inclusion in relation to MSI suggests that mainstream educational settings provide opportunities for increased peer interaction, but there are concerns regarding differentiation practices, such as withdrawal for one-to-one teaching, and their impact on socialization. More importantly, it has been found that increased peer interaction is not necessarily associated with the development of durable peer relationships, as the latter seem to be significantly limited for children with MSI regardless of educational setting. The lack of stable social

Table 2.3 Late twentieth century: key learning points

- Research from the UK reviewed here covers a variety of topics, including surveys of the population with MSI, assessment, communication development, curriculum access, haptic strategies and the use of touch.
- UK research suggests that the field of MSI started to grow in the 1990s with relevant providers starting to develop specialized services and staff training, and special schools played a key role in this process, as they were the commonest type of placement for children with MSI.
- Research from the US reviewed here focuses on inclusion in mainstream settings and various interventions for enhancing peer relationships and communication.
- US research on mainstream settings confirms that mere mainstream placement is not enough for full social inclusion, but the quantitative methods used in most studies did not capture in depth some aspects of social inclusion such as the nature of peer relationships.

networks with peers is apparent in the tendency of children with MSI to spend leisure time with family members instead of friends. Studies have stressed the role of parents, peers and teachers for the success of mainstream placement and evidence from a range of contexts, including school, family, and community, suggests that social inclusion depends on the interplay between numerous environmental factors, such as a school that caters for specific visual, hearing and mobility needs, and appropriately educated communication partners. Consequently, several interventions have focused on providing peer support, assistance with communication or appropriate social conditions for reciprocal interaction to occur. Last but not least, the most important point to make here is that the predominantly quantitative methodologies in the research produced during this period fell short of capturing the nature of peer relationships developed in educational settings, as well as the individual and contextual factors that influence their formation and maintenance.

2.3 Research in the twenty-first century: across the globe

In this section, I present in detail studies published in England as a case study and also a selection of studies carried out internationally. The presentation of studies here has been structured according to chronological order and topic explored, whereby studies on the same topics or similar themes have been grouped together. It is helpful to stress here, that this section of Chapter 2 is heavily research-focused, which is why I clearly summarize each research study by referring to the topic and research questions explored, main methods used, the key findings, and, where relevant, I highlight any gaps and/or weaknesses that warrant further research. I have decided to adopt this style for this section that reviews more recent research, in order to provide a useful up-to-date resource to all those currently conducting research on MSI and education, either at undergraduate or postgraduate level. It is worth advising the readers, who might not be interested in those detailed research summaries, to skip this part of the book, and proceed to the rest of the chapters that focus more heavily on theory and practice.

2.3.1 England and the UK

Together with colleagues, I recently conducted a scoping review of research studies published in England over the past 20 years on MSI and education (see Kamenopoulou et al. 2021). We identified 29 relevant studies and analysed them by: 1) terminology used, 2) topics explored, and 3) methodologies adopted. We found that in the English context the term MSI has come to overlap with other labels that are poorly defined and understood, a finding which has important implications for both research and practice. Secondly, we found very little research into mainstream settings and research including learners' voices. The most researched topic was communication (assessment and interventions), followed by strategies based on senses other than vision and hearing. Finally, we found a lack of consistency and transparency in how methodologies were reported with key information about participant characteristics, sample size and other aspects of the research design often missing from the published research articles or reports. Here, I discuss in detail these and other studies from England that have been published since or that did not meet the criteria for inclusion in our scoping review.

Communication

Taylor (2007) explored the participation of children with MSI in *child-centred planning*, with a particular focus on how the profiles of children with MSI influence the process of eliciting their voices and experiences. Participants for this study were three children with MSI, who were chosen as representative examples of the range of needs that pupils with MSI might have, and who used very different methods of communication. Based on the findings, the author recommended strategies that can support a better understanding of the voices of children with MSI, including the need for: *tailoring the process to each child's strengths and weaknesses*, using *communication supports* suitable for children with MSI (such as objects), professionals carrying out assessment and interviews with the children to have *prior knowledge* of the child, an *environment* in which children feel comfortable (such as their classroom), and finally, *triangulation* or cross-checking of information gathered from the children with other data such as school records and observations.

Goldbart and Caton (2010) collected the views of professionals, family members, researchers and practitioners on the most effective *communication methods* for children with complex needs (including S/PMLD, severe ASD, and

ASD accompanied by challenging behaviour, but without specifying if this included MSI. Additionally, they conducted a literature review and used data from a survey previously completed by speech and language therapists. Their findings showed support for the use of approaches consisting of recording basic information about the person's communication needs and preferences, such as the *communication passport* and the communication *dictionary*, which can be easily accessed by all possible interactive partners. They also found the *intensive interaction* approach (Nind 2008) to be commonly used and to be underpinned by an increasing evidence base (I provide a summary of the evidence base available on intensive interaction in Chapter 4). Communication systems based on *symbols*, such as the Picture Exchange Communication System (PECS) were also mentioned (see section 2.3.2), but the need for professionals to be trained in the use of symbol-based approaches was emphasized. Finally, the approach with the largest evidence base demonstrating its effectiveness was the use of *cause* and *effect* activities, including the use of devices with *switches*.

In subsequent studies, Goldbart et al. (2014) surveyed speech and language therapists about their reasons for choosing communication assessment tools and interventions for children with complex needs, in order to find out if their choices depend on their knowledge of the relevant evidence base. The questionnaire was completed by 55 professionals and the findings revealed that the most commonly used interventions were *intensive interaction and objects of reference*. Interestingly, there was little evidence that professionals chose interventions, based on their knowledge of research evidence supporting their effectiveness, which resulted in great variation in existing practices. In what seems to be a further analysis of the same questionnaire data, Chadwick et al. (2019) investigated which methods are mostly used by speech and language therapists for the *assessment of communication* in children and adults with PMLD, and why. They found that both published and unpublished assessments were used, with many professionals stating that they often used a mixture of both approaches. The non-published assessment methods used fell under the following categories: 1) those created locally with input from the teachers themselves, based on trial and error and years of experience, and 2) tools adapted from existing published assessments. Moreover, formal and informal observations were most commonly used in assessment based on unpublished tools. Findings suggest that the communicative profiles of people with complex needs are unique, hence no single method for the assessment of communication can be sufficient. On the contrary, a combination of formal and informal methods will almost certainly be required.

Taylor and Preece (2010) examined the possibility of adapting the TEACCH approach (Treatment and Education of Autistic and related Communication Handicapped Children) for use with MDVI children (one of them had MSI). TEACCH is a structured approach with four main elements: 1) structuring the environment to make it meaningful for the student, 2) daily schedules using visual timetables, 3) tools to remind the student what will happen next and for how long, and 4) use of visual strategies to demonstrate to students how to successfully carry out activities. It was developed for people with ASD and no vision impairment, hence in this study the researchers had to adapt the visual elements of TEACCH to meet the needs of children with MSI (for example tactile schedules or use of tangible objects). It is important to note that this work was not underpinned by research, but on practitioner reflections and informal observations during work with three young people. Using elements of TEACCH with these three students was generally described as successful, with improvement noted in both receptive and expressive communication, as well as increased independence, but several challenges relating to its implementation were noted, namely that it is not appropriate for students with severe physical impairments and/or limited fine motor skills, who might find it difficult to physically manipulate objects, and that it requires a lot of space and time for planning and development of activities, staff to be trained in its use, and flexibility and adaptations for students with different needs.

Harding et al. (2011) explored the development and use of an intervention using alternative and augmentative communication (AAC) in order to reduce isolation and develop choice-making in two 6-year-old children with PMLD (one of them had VI). AAC refers to a range of high- and low-tech approaches, which may include assistive technology, but it needs to be stressed that the main focus is on interaction and communication and not on technology: 'AAC users typically use a range of modes to support their communication, for example facial expression, gesture, objects, symbols, speech approximations, signs, communication passports and electronic devices' (Harding et al. 2011: 120). After a three-week assessment period, each child received a total of 12.5 hours of one-to-one sessions of AAC implementation involving objects of reference, gestures and signs, over a period of five weeks. The sessions were recorded and coded using an observation matrix, focusing on four areas: comprehension, social interaction, expression and behaviour. The quantitative analysis of the coded observation data demonstrated benefits for both students in relation to communication, but dependent on a thorough language and communication assessment prior to the intervention, as well as good knowledge of the children's functional communication and areas of strength. The authors stressed that the assessment took into consideration information from multiple sources and informal methods, given the children's complex communication needs.

Bunning et al. (2013) explored the *communication interface* between four 12- to 15-year-old students with PMLD (all of them had VI) and their teachers during structured school time. They conducted an in-depth observational study of dyadic interactions that were video-recorded, transcribed and analysed using a coding framework based on structural-functional linguistics, to establish the quality of the observed interactions, focusing on linguistic moves (e.g. initiation or response), functions (e.g. requesting or expressing something) and communicative modalities (e.g. vocalization or gesture). Moreover, the contributions of each member of the dyad during interactions were examined. Findings showed that both children and teachers were able to make contributions to the interactions, although the teachers made more initiations, follow-ups and requests than the students, who responded more and the purpose of their communicative behaviours was most often 'self-expression'. Interestingly, both teachers used speech accompanied by touch and objects, whereas the students favoured vocalization and gesture. The authors stressed that from a structural-functional linguistics theoretical perspective, teachers must consider the role that their understanding of the child's communicative profile plays in successful interactions, as well as the importance of their ability to scaffold interactions appropriately, when the children's communication repertoire is limited, and when they are in a special setting, where more able peers are absent.

Brigg et al. (2016) explored an underresearched topic – i.e. the importance of *humour and laughter* in the context of communication and children with profound disabilities. They observed four 6- to 10-year-old children with PMLD (one of them had VI) during school time and drama workshops. Several qualitative observations of each child were conducted and field notes were used to produce vignettes representing episodes of laughter and humour. Based on the vignettes, the authors reflected on the philosophical meaning of the interactions observed and their importance for the lives of people, for whom verbal communication is severely restricted or completely absent. Their study revealed that the children were fully sharing in the jokes and participating to the same extent as their adult interactive partners, which requires complex cognitive, social and affective abilities. The authors stressed the importance of a safe environment, where the child feels able to participate in jokes, and of adults rejecting negative and stereotypical perceptions of children with profound disabilities; having the time and space to understand and respond to the nuances of a child's communicative repertoire; and recognizing humour as integral to children's communication and connection with other human beings.

Hitchins and Hogan (2018) examined the impact of an individualized auditory verbal (AV) intervention programme on the language development of 129 preschool children with deafness/hearing impairment (with and without additional needs, of whom seven had VI). AV focuses on maximizing the use of hearing technology, so that the child can learn to access sound when communicating. It is different from *oralism*, in that it does not rely on other senses, such as vision for lip-reading and it is delivered through play-based therapy sessions by parents, who are at the heart of the intervention. Their findings showed that those children with additional needs, including MSI, who took part in the intervention for more than two years (with 20 AV intervention sessions per year) saw significant improvement in both their receptive and expressive communication, and highlighted the importance of appropriate early intervention, especially for this group of children.

In a reflective piece, Ellinor (2019) explored the use of *dramatherapy* group workshops for families of children with PMLD. Participants in the workshops were four 7- to 10-year-old children (one of them had HI), their four primary caregivers, one qualified drama therapist and one teaching professional. The aim of the workshops was to provide parents and children with a secure space to share their experiences and explore new ways of relating to each other. Feedback from parents suggested that they benefited from the opportunity to meet and talk with other parents and to interact with their child in a playful manner, free from the practicalities and medical tasks that their everyday interactions usually involve. Children were also able to find flexible and creative ways of negotiating their difficulties when relating to others in the group. The drama therapist leading the group stressed the importance of having a close working relationship with a teacher experienced in working with children with complex needs, and the role of the school's commitment in supporting such collaborative initiatives by investing in appropriate staff and resources.

Pearlman and Michaels (2019) conducted a study focused on *including the voices* of young people with learning disabilities during the EHCP process. They developed a questionnaire, informed by AAC methods, which was used to interview 22 young people (from 7 to 14 years old) with severe, moderate, profound and multiple learning disabilities (without specifying if this included MSI). The interviews focused on the young people's lives at school and home, were video recorded and the interpretations of the young people's communicative behaviours were double-checked by significant adults in their lives (i.e. parents and professionals), who were shown excerpts of the videos. Results showed that the combination of structured interview and AAC approaches allowed the young people to express their views, likes, dislikes and in some cases, aspirations for the future, and when used alongside video recordings, they have the potential to transform the way young people with complex needs are included in the EHCP process. Interestingly, they found differences between the parents and professionals in the interpretation of the young people's behaviours, which is why they stress that it is essential to triangulate feedback from many sources concerning the young person's communicative behaviours.

Inclusive settings

Lacey (2001) explored *the role of* learning support assistants (LSAs) in supporting children with S/PMLD in inclusive settings (without specifically mentioning if any of the children participating in the study had MSI). After mapping inclusive provision available for this group of pupils, she selected schools (N = 24) that were representative of the continuum of provision identified, and collected data by observing the pupils (N = 53), interviewing some of them (N = 13), and also by observing and interviewing LSAs (N = 43), teachers (N = 25) and some parents (N = 30). First, she identified many different types of 'inclusive placements' for this population, such as for example a special school with part of the week being spent in a mainstream school (or with mainstream peers coming into the special school), as well as mainstream school with (or without) withdrawal for specialized support. The most inclusive scenario was a resourced class in a mainstream school (with pupils joining their class groups for some lessons but also spending time in the resourced class with other pupils with S/PMLD). Second, she found that LSAs were crucial in terms of planning and offering opportunities for peer interaction in both mainstream and special settings. However, some LSAs mentioned important challenges they faced in their role, including: 1) negative teacher and/or school attitudes, 2) lack of communication on the part of the teachers and lack of time for meeting and planning together, 3) ambiguity about their role, and 4) being given full responsibility for the children they support instead of being responsible for supporting the teacher, an issue that was also linked to them feeling underpaid for a job that requires specialized skills (supporting students with complex needs). Although these are generic issues that support staff have been consistently reported to face by research in the UK and other countries, this study raises the question of whether or not children with S/PMLD in mainstream schools are getting the best possible support, and it emphasizes that the correct deployment of LSAs is critical in these contexts.

A study conducted by Sense (2002) explored the *social inclusion* of deafblind children and young people in the UK, with a view to evaluating the opportunities for participation in social activities outside school hours. The scope of this research therefore goes beyond the school setting, exploring the ability of society as a context where interaction takes place, to actively include all its members. However, the relevance of the findings and the inclusive methodology employed render it worthy of mention. In terms of methodology, the voices of the children and young people were included in the survey, in addition to those of their parents. The findings revealed that deafblind children and young people spent leisure time isolated from the wider social world, since close family members were often the only source of social experiences outside school hours. More importantly, the main reasons reducing opportunities for social participation were related to obstacles in communication and mobility, which limited independence and rendered most social activities inaccessible.

Kamenopoulou (2012) explored the *social inclusion* of four deafblind young people placed in mainstream secondary schools, focusing on the quantity and quality of their peer interactions and relationships, and using the framework of Bronfenbrenner's ecological systems theory (see Chapter 3). She conducted semi-structured observations of breaktimes during one school week per case study, and interviewed staff (both general classroom teachers and specialized staff, i.e. two staff per case study), the parents (one per case study) and the four deafblind young people. Before their interview, teachers also completed a semi-structured questionnaire about the young person's amount and nature of peer interactions and relationships at school. It was found that the young people were socially present in their schools, but several obstacles to their full social inclusion were also identified. The obstacles were related to the school microsystem (e.g. withdrawal from lessons for one-to-one support had a negative impact on socialization), the family–school liaison or mesosystem (e.g. parents feeling that their concerns about their child being bullied were not addressed by the teachers), and the young people's characteristics or biosystem (e.g. degree of functioning vision and hearing, lack of age-appropriate social skills). Factors enabling socialization and positive social outcomes were also identified, including: early assessment and identification of needs, adequate preparation of all school staff and peers in relation to the young person's specific communication needs, and smooth collaboration and knowledge exchange between special and general teaching staff, and between family and school. I refer to this study further in Chapter 4 when discussing strategies to support social and emotional development.

Multisensory approaches

Miller (2001) examined the use of interactive technology in the context of multisensory environments and identified good practice within both mainstream and special settings. She conducted five case studies of schools in different geographical areas in the UK, and collected data by interviewing 15 school-based professionals (both in an initial focus group and also individually following the observation of their lessons), by observing and filming teaching sessions, and by collecting and analysing documents such as lesson plans and curricula. Findings highlighted the importance of developing and improving staff expertise and confidence, especially in using interactive technologies. Other prerequisites for the effective use of interactive technology in multisensory environments included: funding for adequate resources and staffing, appropriate space, and technical backup; also, clarity of purpose (staff to be clear how technology will be used to meet subject-specific curriculum targets), understanding of learners' individualized methods of communication and matching these to the technology available (for example choosing appropriate devices, such as switches), and the development of systems for recording children's needs that can be easily shared between school staff. Last but not least, an unexpected finding was that multisensory rooms were used not only in special schools and for learners with the most profound needs, but also in mainstream schools and for pupils with a wider range of needs.

Park (2004) conducted a study on *interactive storytelling* with a group of learners with profound and multiple needs, including MSI. He ran a series of 45-minute poetry workshops with stories adapted from the Book of Genesis over the course of eight weeks. Participants were 11 children and at least six members of staff from the same special school. The workshop started with a ten-minute introductory activity (like circle time, in which each participant's name was called and repeated by the group with accompanying sound and rhythm), followed by the reading and repeating of the story, again accompanied by sound and rhythm. Feedback by staff suggested that the intervention was experienced positively by the children, who were participating and having fun. Staff mentioned the need for each child to have their own device for communicating throughout the week (not just for the storytelling session) and the important distinction between context-specific (e.g. 'hello' or 'goodbye') and context-free switch messages (e.g. sound effects), which can be used more flexibly. It is interesting to note that after participating in the intervention, the staff became more confident and proactive in adapting many other stories, such as tales from around the world, and created interactive versions accessible to learners with complex needs.

Preece and Zhao (2015) also explored how multisensory stories are used for a range of children with complex needs, including MSI in different types of educational placement, and the factors affecting their use. They selected five schools and conducted observations of multisensory story sessions (N = 18) and interviewed school-based professionals (N = 27). Across the schools, there was great variation in how stories were used, and most importantly, they were not only used as interventions to address specific needs, but in many other ways, such as to keep children entertained during free time. Teachers reported adapting the original stories and mixing and matching objects intended for specific stories. Based on their findings they challenged the idea that specific guidelines for the correct use of multisensory stories should always be followed and stressed the need for flexibility in how stories are used, depending on multiple factors affecting each individual case. For example, they pointed out that a specific story might be experienced as enjoyable by one child at one point in time, but not always, depending for example on their medical conditions or other interventions they receive during the school day – and, more importantly, that different stories and ways of using them are appropriate for different children.

Learning styles and characteristics

Hodges (2004) explored the concept of learning styles and its relevance to the education of deafblind children. She conducted a survey completed by teachers of deafblind children, as well as other professionals with responsibility for assessment (N = 61) on the practice of assessment and case studies of deafblind children (N = 14). Findings revealed that teachers prefer informal observation to the use of published assessment tools, and that they may not know what learning style is and how to assess it. The case studies involved interviews with the teachers and observation of taught tasks, and demonstrated that despite their commonality (deafblindness), the children had their own learning styles and that taking these into consideration when teaching can lead to better learning outcomes. Importantly, the results of the case studies challenged commonly accepted ideas in relation to what is good pedagogy for deafblind learners, namely: 1) that priority needs to be given to communication over other skills like for example independence and self-help skills; 2) the idea that the use of familiar stimuli should be favoured; and 3) the need for constant structure and routine. The author pointed out that these practices are commonly accepted as suitable for deafblind learners without being based on evidence, but on views widely held by practitioners.

Deuce et al. (2012) focused on those children and young people with deafblindness caused by CHARGE syndrome and explored the *impact of CHARGE* on function and learning. A questionnaire was completed by families (N = 44) focusing on diagnosis, child development and educational provision. The published piece of research was limited to a presentation of findings relating to the first topic (i.e. diagnosis) and highlighted the complexity of the condition and the various medical problems that accompany it. Based on their findings, they stressed the importance of transdisciplinary and multi-agency collaboration when identifying and supporting children with CHARGE, and the need for all the professionals involved to be knowledgeable about the syndrome and the specific challenges associated with it (such as for example sleep and eating difficulties that were commonly reported by families).

In a subsequent study, Deuce (2017) focused on the *learning characteristics* of children with CHARGE syndrome, in order to help develop an effective pedagogy for this subgroup of learners with MSI. She analysed 58 educational reports of children, administered a questionnaire that was completed by 52 teachers, and interviewed 11 practitioners experienced in children with CHARGE based at the Perkins School for the Blind in the US. She identified numerous characteristics of learners with CHARGE that are common in the wider deafblind population such as: 1) requiring additional time to process information, 2) preferring different communication methods for expressive and receptive communication, 3) greater difficulty in forming relationships with peers than with adults, 4) difficulty in empathizing with peers and in understanding and expressing their own emotional states, and 5) dependence on routines and structure. However, she also found some distinct characteristics for this group such as: 1) a combination of sensory impairments in most if not all senses, 2) sensory integration difficulties and poor self-regulation, 3) high levels of fatigue, stress and anxiety, and 4) poor fine motor and handwriting skills. However, the research also found that this distinct subgroup benefits from the same strategies as the rest of the deafblind population, and stressed that successful use of strategies is dependent on: 1) staff being knowledgeable and skilled in supporting their needs, 2) the school ethos and perceptions of staff about what might be suitable for each learner, and 3) practical issues to do with implementing strategies within the school day. Interestingly, she also found that in mainstream schools, fewer and less useful strategies were employed.

Musical development

Ockelford and colleagues have been researching and mapping the musical development of children with S/PMLD and have shown that musical education can enhance their development and wider curriculum, because it enriches their personal and educational environments. Based on their work, they have developed 'Sounds of Intent', a framework of musical development in children with S/PMLD with two strands: 1) activities undertaken for their intrinsic musical value, and 2) activities that advance learning and development (Ockelford 2000). In a subsequent study, Ockelford et al. (2005) explored the possible uses of this framework for children with PMLD (without specifying if this included MSI) by analysing teachers' observations of individual pupils in special schools for a period of 24 months. Based on their findings, they suggested the creation of an interactive version on a tablet/PC, which could be used in the classroom or other contexts in order to assess and enhance musical development and to allow direct recording of the child's progress.

Following the development of an observation schedule based on the Sounds of Intent developmental framework, Ockelford et al. (2011) carried out a six-month intervention study in a special school with 20 pupils with S/PMLD (all of them had VI). The pupils took part in specially designed musical activities and their level of engagement was observed and recorded. They concluded that while music-developmental progress is possible for learners with S/PMLD, it will be small and gradual, and also that without specialist musical intervention, musical progress is likely to be minimal. Lastly, they noted that further research is required to determine the extent to which other context-specific factors might have influenced the children's musical progress, in addition to the musical intervention.

Haptic strategies

McLinden and colleagues have explored the role of *haptic learning strategies* in children with MDVI or VI and complex needs/additional needs. One of their foci has been the use of the Moon tactile code for enabling access to literacy. The Moon code is a tactile method for reading (like Braille that uses dots), comprising raised letters similar to the Latin alphabet, but simplified. In a reflective piece, McCall and McLinden (2001) argued for the benefits of using this method with this group of learners not just for developing reading and writing skills, but for providing them with the opportunity to take part in literacy experiences. For example, children can use Moon to increase their independence, interact with peers more fully in lessons, and make use of skills that may have remained hidden otherwise, such as simple phonic skills. They also usefully noted that any evaluation of literacy skills must consider the wider context shaping children's learning as well as the expectations of their schools, teachers and significant others. In a subsequent study exploring teachers' perspectives on the use of Moon to develop literacy for children with VI and additional disabilities, McCall and McLinden (2007) highlighted some of the reasons for adopting the Moon code reported by teachers (for example increased confidence) and also some of its disadvantages (for example lack of ready-made resources in Moon). While the researchers intended to examine the development of literacy skills through the use of Moon, they also illuminated benefits in other areas, such as social inclusion, independence and self-esteem, since the code can enable participation in activities of an abstract nature.

To explore haptic learning strategies more systematically, McLinden (2004) conducted an observation study of nine children with VI and additional disabilities interacting with old and new objects in different contexts within the school, and followed up observations with teacher interviews. Their findings highlighted the importance of observing a child's interaction with different objects, textures and shapes, to better understand their haptic abilities, and to design appropriate interventions and educational programmes. McLinden (2012) further expanded his review of literature on haptic mediating strategies for children with VI and intellectual disabilities, and stressed that vision plays an important part in assisting haptic learning experiences, but also that the adult's role is crucial in adapting the intervention and environment to the child's individual needs. Accordingly, he called for more research to evaluate and develop mediating indicators depending on children's needs.

In their most recently published work, McLinden and colleagues focused on the *role of the specialist teachers* for children with VI and multiple disabilities, which they conceptualized from a bioecological systems theory (BST) perspective (Bronfenbrenner 1979, 2005). Their focus was on the role of the teacher in supporting individual development, which they argued is influenced and shaped by continuous interactions between a person's characteristics and complex eco-systemic factors, and I mention this work again in Chapter 3 that critically discusses relevant theoretical perspectives.

Olfactory strategies

Solomons (2005) researched the use of aromatherapy massage to develop shared attention behaviours in children in the autistic spectrum with severe learning difficulties (without specifying if this included MSI). The intervention involved use of smell and touch during aromatherapy massage sessions introduced in the school routines of four children attending a special school, in order to support the development of their sensory system, including their awareness of self and others. The children received a massage twice a week for eight months and each child was observed during the massage session once per month. Teachers and parents were interviewed before and after the intervention and during the intervention; the children were also observed once per month taking part in a sensory exploration activity involving objects with an adult. Despite the methodological limitations of this study that may have affected the results, such as for example the small duration of the intervention or the familiarity between the children and the staff delivering the massage, it nevertheless found evidence of increased shared attention behaviours like eye contact, pointing at objects following the intervention, and also increased effectiveness of the aromatherapy massage intervention compared to the sensory exploration activity.

Murdoch et al. (2014) explored the use of fragrances for choice making during mealtimes. They carried out case studies of three deafblind children and used mixed methods to assess the children's choice-making prior to, during and after the intervention. They interviewed the students' keyworkers and other teaching and therapy staff, conducted video observations of the students' free choices during mealtimes, and analysed keyworkers' daily records of their choice-making behaviours. They found that students responded positively to fragrances and that their confidence in making choices and expressing their preferences during mealtimes had increased. They also noted that using a fragranced pen for delivering the scents was a successful way of doing olfactory work with these children in a safe way. Finally, in terms of areas for future research, they stressed that more work needs to be done on the number of fragrances that can be used in a single session without causing the students to feel overloaded with olfactory information.

Visual strategies

Little and Dutton (2015) explored the use of coloured tents to engage children with multiple disabilities and visual impairment (MDVI). They designed the coloured tents in order to remove unnecessary visual and auditory input from the environment (such as patterns, noise, clutter) and to enhance the ability of the children to concentrate and use their remaining vision. They tested this intervention with one child (9 years) and one young person (17 years), who received focused sensory sessions in the coloured tents over a period of two years. They evaluated the intervention weekly using video recordings of the sessions that were discussed in staff meetings. They found that with the removal of unnecessary distractions, students' concentration, motivation and engagement increased, and also their communication improved. In a subsequent study, Pilling and Little (2020) conducted a feasibility study to evaluate the role of coloured tents in stimulating vision for children with MDVI, and more specifically if they cause changes in visual behaviour, and under what circumstances. The participants in this study were nine primary aged children, whose visual attention was measured before and after entering the tent and their behaviours during their time spent in the tent were also recorded once per week over a period of four weeks. They found that for the intervention to be effective many repeated sessions in the tent were necessary.

Summary

Again, most studies in England since 2000 to the present day have been conducted in special schools by special education practitioners. As I explained in the previous section, this approach is the opposite of the one adopted by research (and practice) from other countries, such as the US, that have paid far more attention to interventions in mainstream schools. Additionally, most studies are primarily based on data collected through observations of case study children and/or some discussions with teaching professionals. The views of the parents and children/young people themselves have been sought much less. Although the difficulties of engaging vulnerable participants in research are uncontested (for a helpful discussion of the reasons why it is challenging to successfully engage participants with profound and complex disabilities in research, see Imray and Colley 2017), it can be argued that this is a huge gap in the current evidence base that informs policy and practice.

Table 2.4 Research in the twenty-first century in England: key learning points

- The term MSI overlaps with other labels, examples of which are S/PMLD, MDVI, profound and multiple disabilities, hearing impairment and additional needs.
- Most research studies on MSI in this context have focused on communication, but a range of interventions have also been explored.
- A common theme identified from the studies reviewed here is that professionals must be flexible and adaptable, and that multidisciplinary work is crucial.
- The majority of studies have focused on special settings and used adults (i.e. teachers, other professionals and parents) as main sources of data and observations (rather than interviews) when collecting data on children. A lot more research is needed on children's voices and in mainstream settings.

2.3.2 International

International research on multisensory impairment over the last two decades is again dominated by the US, but there is also a steady and notable body of significant research being produced in other countries, especially in the Netherlands and some of the Nordic countries, including Denmark and Sweden. In this section I do not provide a holistic review of international literature, but will discuss a few selected studies.

In a study from Sweden, Möller and Danermark (2007) surveyed 34 deafblind students to identify personal and environmental *barriers to participation* in secondary upper schools. The young people mentioned environmental factors that impeded their participation, including bad lighting conditions and poor labelling of school areas, difficulties with transport to and from the school, as well as issues to do with their participation in activities such as physical education (PE). Young people also noted that it is important that people in the school setting have knowledge of deafblindness so that they are aware of the need for special attention during interactions. This study stresses the role of the school environment in including deafblind pupils by addressing their very specific needs in relation to communication and mobility. Accordingly, the authors argue that deafblindness does play a significant role, but the context can be designed appropriately to address differences and to allow full participation.

In Denmark, Dammeyer (2014) carried out a holistic review of *public health issues* related to deafblindness across the lifespan. He concluded that there is an association between deafblindness and several health-related issues, including mental health problems and 'behavioral disorders' (Dammeyer 2014: 558), and suggested that this may be due to both biological factors linked to the cause of deafblindness or to the psychological impact of sensory deprivation. However, he also usefully highlighted the difficulties with assessment of co-morbid disorders (such as autism for example) when the person is deafblind, which might lead to both over- and under-identification. Finally, he stressed the need for more research on this topic, to be able to offer the best support to people with deafblindness.

Studies from the Netherlands have explored varied topics. Van Der Putten et al. (2005) used a quasi-experimental pre-test/post-test with control group design to evaluate the implementation of a curriculum that aims to develop independence by focusing on functional movement skills. This is an American curriculum called Mobility Opportunities Via Education (MOVE). Participants were 44 children and young people with profound multiple disabilities (PMD) aged 2–16 years attending seven centres for special education across the country. All had an SLD, very limited (or no) use of their hands and arms, and additional 'sensory disorders' (Van Der Putten et al. 2005: 614). Results showed that the level of independence of the experimental group ($N = 32$) during movement activities increased significantly more compared to the control group ($N = 12$) that showed little progress.

Vervloed et al. (2006) conducted a case study of *teacher–child interactions* in the context of congenital deafblindness. The focus of the study was the interaction between a toddler aged 3 years and 4 months and his teacher. Researchers collected data during three activities that provided opportunities for close interaction, i.e. bathing, dressing and playing with favourite objects. These activities were part of the child's daily routine and curriculum, aimed at supporting successful interactions and memory processes. The researchers recorded video of teacher–pupil interactions once a week and once a fortnight over a period of four months, gathering a total of 16 hours of recorded interactions and analysed data statistically using a structured coding system. Their first important finding was that only 2 per cent of the total 16 hours recorded were of interactions long enough to qualify for inclusion in the data analysed, since one of the criteria for inclusion was that interactions had to last 'at least several seconds' (Vervloed et al. 2006: 338). They also found that the teacher was initiating more interactions than allowing the child to lead on interactions, which was not unexpected given the child's age and stage of development. However, the authors cite research on the interactions of deaf children and their parents showing that the more domineering style of communication often found in the latter tends to impede or slow down language development. Their recommendations include increasing interaction time between the child and their parents, as well as teachers, improving the teachers' responsiveness to the child's initiations and them being able to give the child more independence to initiate interactions – just like adults do for typically developing children, who explore the world and satisfy their curiosity without adult support.

Tadema et al. (2008) carried out three case studies to explore the implementation of a new *specialized curriculum* for children with profound intellectual and multiple disabilities (including VI) that was implemented in the Netherlands following the adoption of legislation in 2003 that led to increasing numbers of children with complex needs accessing educational settings. The core principles underpinning the curriculum are flexibility depending on each child's profile and an initial holistic assessment by a range of experts in a collaborative way. The assessment provides the basis for setting goals that can be broken down into smaller targets (i.e. short-term, mid-term and long-term). The idea is that when the child meets the short-term goals, this then leads to the acquisition of the mid-term goals and so on. Regular evaluation of the goals is also done collaboratively by a range of experts. In this study, three special schools took part, with five students from each school being the focus of the case study ($N = 15$ in total). The researchers used a protocol to guide data collection, which comprised mixed methods, including documents, questionnaires, evaluation forms and observation. The first notable finding was that although all schools had received the same training on the curriculum, each operationalized it differently. An important factor that played a role in the successful implementation of the curriculum was the degree to which staff worked collaboratively and supported each other. They moreover identified that teachers had difficulty with setting goals for their students, hence they argued that more training on this specific aspect would be beneficial.

Haakma et al. (2016) conducted a multiple case study to explore the link between motivation in students with acquired MSI and teacher behaviours that they called 'need supportive', i.e. tailored to the needs of this specific group, such as coming to terms with MSI that changes over time, which is the case of those with Usher's syndrome. Participants were three students and three of their teachers, while two of the students were in a special setting, and one was in mainstream school. Teacher–pupil interactions during specific activities were recorded once or twice per week over a two-month period and selected fragments of the interactions were coded according to observation categories predetermined based on the literature about supportive teacher behaviours and student engagement. Overall, the study found evidence that there was higher student engagement when teacher–pupil interactions support 'students' need for competence, autonomy and relatedness' (Haakma et al. 2016: 324). These are the three psychological needs that all students have in common, according to self-determination theory, and the authors explained that these can be met if teachers provide structure, and support for autonomy and involvement. Finally, the researchers usefully noted that future research should also focus on peer interactions.

In the US, Ali et al. (2011) explored the effectiveness of PECS when combined with tangible symbols for teaching students with vision impairment and multiple disabilities to make requests. PECS is one of the existing AAC systems and it was initially designed to teach people with autism and cognitive disabilities to communicate using single pictures and then multiple picture sentences. Participants were four students with a combination of different disabilities in addition to VI and limited communication skills. The research focused more specifically on the following questions: if students can learn requesting skills using this approach, if they can generalize those skills to other contexts within the school, and if the skills learned are maintained over time. It was found that using adapted PECS can be an effective way of teaching students with vision impairment and multiple disabilities to make requests, and that they generalize and maintain this skill across contexts and over time.

Bruce and Borders (2015) synthesized *international theory, research, and practice* in relation to children who are deaf and have additional disabilities, including those who are deafblind. In relation to the latter group, they found that the most frequently researched topic is communication (which is in line with the findings in relation to research in England that I discussed in the previous section) and that there is evidence for the effectiveness of interventions informed by both child-centred approaches (such as the van Dijk Curricular Approach, which focuses for example on the development of attachment and trust between adult and child), and also systematic approaches grounded in behaviourism. Moreover, they found ample evidence that tangible symbols are effective, especially for pre-linguistic deafblind children, as well as a range of tactile approaches. Furthermore, in relation to communication, the review identified evidence for the importance of interventions tailored to each individual's communication level, which also consider the context of the interaction and place emphasis on daily interactions taking place within natural settings. Interestingly, they also found that in the field of deafblindness, the notions of literacy and literacy-rich environments are perceived by educators in flexible and creative ways, who make use of different materials and approaches that go beyond what has traditionally been considered literacy (i.e. reading and writing).

In a subsequent study, Bruce et al. (2016) focused more specifically on reviewing work conducted between 1990 and 2015 on communication and literacy in relation to deafblind children and young people (0–22 years). In relation to communication, they found that most research has explored expressive communication and that more work is needed in relation to receptive communication and comprehension in children who are deafblind. In relation to literacy, they identified a gap in knowledge about emergent literacy and interventions for reading and writing with children who are deafblind.

Hartmann and Weismer (2016) reviewed international literature on the use of technology when teaching children who are deafblind, focusing on three different theoretical frameworks for incorporating technology, including Universal Design for Learning (UDL). They stressed that UDL is an effective approach, because it allows the flexibility and creativity required for engaging deafblind learners (I discuss UDL and its effectiveness in ensuring access and inclusion in more detail in Chapter 4). However, despite the fact that there is strong evidence to suggest that technology is beneficial for deafblind children, the researchers pointed out that there is overall limited guidance for professionals on how to implement specific technology tools that have been found to be effective.

Hartshorne and Schmittel (2016) focused on social and emotional development, examining the literature in relation to attachment, empathy and friendships in children who are deafblind. They also discussed the factors that place deafblind children at risk for poor social and emotional outcomes and development, including 'genetic risk, sensory impairment, family stress, lack of resources, challenging behaviour, and problems with self-regulation and self-monitoring' (Hartshorne and Schmittel 2016: 446). Finally, they considered the benefits of mainstream settings in terms of providing opportunities for peer interaction that can help shape emotional and social development in deafblind children. In relation to this, they did however point out that mere mainstream placement does not necessarily lead to increased interactions or more friendships, hence they stressed the need for targeted interventions, like the use of play, to provide increased opportunities for interaction with peers.

In a final study I have selected to include from the US, Nelson et al. (2016) investigated if three groups of interventions, including 'provision of meaningful, enjoyable, and interactive activities, anticipatory strategies, and calming strategies' (Nelson et al. 2016: 496) would increase self-regulation in one child with deafblindness. They found that all interventions reduced the frequency and duration of dysregulated behaviours, increased active participation in activities, and shortened the periods between a dysregulated and a calm state.

In Brazil, Boas et al. (2016) conducted and recorded observations of a child with congenital deafblindness and their specialized teacher, and they analysed the child's interaction and attention processes. They found that the child showed attention to the interactive partner when activities involved music and rhythm. In relation to non-verbal communication, the child displayed behaviours that included, but were not limited to, vocalizations, touch and body contact. The authors concluded that a significant communication partner, who is able to identify, interpret and respond appropriately to the child's attention and

Table 2.5 International research in the twenty-first century: key learning points

- Here selected studies from various countries were presented, including Sweden, Denmark, the Netherlands, US, Brazil, India and Canada, some of which had a wide – i.e. international – scope.
- Varied topics have been explored, including, but not limited to, communication (which is again the most researched area), specialized curricula, barriers to participation, co-morbidity with mental illness, literacy, use of technology and UDL.
- Main findings from this work include evidence for the effectiveness of tactile approaches, tangible symbols, UDL, staff collaboration, approaches focused on both personal and environmental barriers, flexible and tailored to individual needs.

communicative behaviours, is essential, and that other methods of communication used should be tailored to the individual's characteristics.

A study from Canada that is worth concluding this section with is a global review of literature on participation experiences of people with deafblindness (Jaiswal et al. 2018). Although this study did not include only work focusing on children and young people, but on deafblind people of all ages, it is worth mentioning, because its findings are relevant to children and young people too. The review identified 54 studies that met the criteria for inclusion, and its findings highlighted that regardless of type of MSI, all persons with deafblindness face challenges in 'communication, mobility, daily living functioning and social interactions' (Jaiswal et al. 2018: 27). As a result, they generally have feelings of isolation, insecurity and uncertainty about their future. Moreover, they found that the experiences of participation of deafblind people are influenced by 'dynamic interactions between personal factors (such as onset and type of impairments) and environmental influences (such as attitude, technology, and supports)' (Jaiswal et al. 2018: 27). Finally, they argued that we need a better understanding of deafblind people's participation experiences in order to be able to increase their participation.

It is noteworthy that although the field of MSI is underresearched, there is a growing body of international research focusing on deafblind adults. For those interested in reading more on this specific topic, two examples are worthy of mention. Further to their study mentioned in the previous paragraph, Jaiswal et al. (2020) conducted semi-structured qualitative interviews with 16 deafblind adults (aged 18 and above) in India about their participation experiences and their meanings of participation in society. In Australia, Roy et al. (2021) used a qualitative methodology to engage 15 people with lived experience of deafblindness (aged between 44 and 80 years) in order to co-design and co-produce appropriate intervention approaches. These are just two examples of research that is taking place in the field at the moment that is cutting-edge and informed by participatory approaches, aiming to include the voices of those who have lived experience of deafblindness. What remains to be seen is if these and other approaches will be used in future research focusing on children and young people with MSI, whose voices have thus far remained silenced.

2.4 Concluding notes

Undoubtedly, the Covid-19 pandemic brought about huge changes in people's daily lives and some great challenges, especially for some groups of people, like those with disabilities. After the first lockdowns were imposed in numerous countries around the world, in April 2020, an article in the *New Yorker* (Wright 2020) focused on how the different pandemic-related health measures adopted by several countries were having an impact on deafblind people more specifically. Since deafblind people rely a lot on physical proximity and touch to communicate and to gather information about their environment, measures such as mask wearing, social distancing and use of gloves constitute major barriers. In June 2020, Deafblind International organized a webinar for participants to exchange experiences and solutions to the challenges caused by the pandemic (Wittich et al. 2021). In total, there were 30 submissions to the call for abstracts from 5 continents and 13 countries across the North and South (including Australia, India, the UK, Ireland, the Netherlands, Germany, Norway, Sweden, Mexico, Brazil, the US and Canada), and 26 were selected. They kept field notes during the workshop and thematically analysed them, also cross-checking with the recordings of the presentations that they repeatedly watched. They identified eight themes, as follows: 'access to information, communication, accessibility of services, adaptations to service delivery, online safety and security, physical distancing, mental health and research' (Wittich et al. 2021: 4). I argue that all are relevant to children and young people with MSI in the current global context that has seen significant disruption in education and other services for those with disabilities. In relation to research that is the focus of this chapter, it is important to stress here that 'all researchers agreed that access to and availability of research funding remains a challenge, making the visibility and unique requirements of persons living with deafblindness an ongoing priority' (Wittich et al. 2021: 10). The lack of funding opportunities for research on MSI could be due to the fact that they are a relatively small group worldwide. However, unless more funding is made available for research on MSI, none of the areas for further research identified throughout this chapter can be explored in a way that is meaningful and allows the collection of a strong evidence base for what works best for learners with MSI.

3 Theory: MSI and child development

3.1 Factors affecting the impact of MSI on development

In this chapter, I discuss the impact of MSI on development under two overarching themes: 1) *primary* difficulties or difficulties directly associated with MSI, and 2) *secondary* difficulties, which might subsequently emerge in other areas of development due to the primary difficulties. In order to provide an account of the possible secondary difficulties, I first critically discuss different theoretical frameworks that can be or have been adopted for the conceptualization of development in the context of MSI, and I then argue for the suitability of adopting a bioecological systems theory (BST) framework (Bronfenbrenner and Morris 2006) for the conceptualization of developmental challenges associated with MSI. In the final part of this chapter (and in Chapter 4), I discuss the possible implications of such developmental challenges for education and learning.

Before beginning this chapter, it is worthwhile stressing again that the impact of MSI on development will not be exactly the same across the deafblind population, because it will depend on numerous factors (e.g. time of onset, time of diagnosis, aetiology, nature and combination of vision and hearing impairments, presence or not of other disabilities, interventions employed), all of which influence how each person experiences living with MSI. However, there are some commonalities in the developmental pathways taken by children with MSI so a general developmental pattern can be identified (Clark 2000).

3.2 Impact on child development: primary difficulties

In the literature about MSI (see for example, Aitken 2000b), there is unanimous agreement that the primary difficulties caused by MSI are as follows:

1. Acquiring information about the world, including people.
2. Successfully communicating with others.
3. Moving around independently.

In relation to the first difficulty, i.e. *acquiring information* about the world, children with MSI have reduced input via their distance senses (vision and hearing) and/or have sensory integration difficulties when receiving external input, so they cannot automatically collect information about their surrounding environment in the same way that typically developing children would. For typically developing children, gathering information about spaces, objects and people around them happens naturally and for the most part unconsciously or naturally through their vision and hearing (Murdoch 1997). Children with MSI have limited or no use of these senses so they experience the world in very different terms, for example by relying a lot on their other senses, that is, touch, taste and smell. Given the vital role of both distance senses in providing information about the environment, children with MSI often miss out on information and perceive the environment in a way that is fragmented and not always meaningful or coherent. This is why they often struggle with understanding basic concepts such as that of *time* and *space*. They moreover might need help to develop their *self awareness*, for example understanding their body and its different parts, and their relation to space, objects and other people.

The second difficulty is considered to be the main challenge that people with MSI face, and it is in the area of *communication* and *language development*. Aitken (2000b) explains that in order for successful communication to take place, there are three prerequisites: 1) someone to communicate with, 2) something to communicate about, and 3) a common method of communication between the people interacting. Depending on the type and degree of vision and hearing impairment and other factors (e.g. presence or not of additional disabilities), children with MSI may benefit from a variety of methods of communication and a lot of them, especially the congenitally deafblind, tend to display idiosyncratic behaviours (Miles 1999; Pease 2000). Idiosyncratic behaviours have communicative purpose that is only meaningful or applicable to the specific person and might not be understood by others if they are not familiar with this specific person's behaviours or their meaning/purpose. It is unlikely that all possible interactive partners will be familiar with a specific child's preferred communication method(s) or with the meaning of their idiosyncratic behaviours. Even if the person with MSI uses oral speech to communicate, additional strategies might be required by the interactive partner(s), such as for example, ensuring physical proximity or using tactile cues to compensate for the person's lack of or limited vision and hearing. When interactive partners are not familiar with the method(s) of communication used by the person with MSI or the additional strategies that may help them successfully take part in the interaction, this can lead to communication breakdowns.

The third and final of the primary difficulties refers to the fact that a person with lack of or limited vision and hearing will also have limited ability to move around independently and might therefore feel particularly vulnerable when in unfamiliar surroundings and reluctant to explore them. This becomes immediately apparent if one imagines closing their eyes or switching off the lights in the night and tries to navigate even familiar surroundings or to complete everyday tasks in complete darkness (for a fun activity of this nature, see Chapter 4). As a consequence, *orientation and mobility* will be challenging and the child with MSI will have limited opportunities to independently experience and explore the world, and unless they develop independence skills, they will be to a great extent dependent on others to provide support with moving around, especially when in unfamiliar surroundings.

To sum up, MSI primarily affects a child's ability and chances to successfully gather information about their environment, to communicate with others and to move around independently. Children with MSI will therefore initially be dependent on other people's ability to support, enable and maximize their access to, understanding of and interaction with the outside world, all of which will support and enhance their cognitive development.

3.3 Impact on child development: secondary difficulties

When discussing how MSI affects development, McInnes and Treffry (1982) discuss the impact of the primary difficulties on a child's extrinsic motivation. This means the child has limited access to and perception of the external factors that motivate typically developing children to explore, learn and develop cognitively, but also emotionally and socially. Hence if considered in relation to the primary effects of MSI, possible patterns of secondary difficulties, mostly in the area of social and emotional development can be anticipated, such as for example: low self-esteem and lack of motivation, delayed social skills development, and difficulty in maintaining social interactions and relationships.

Difficulties in communication are as I explained the biggest challenge that children with MSI face, because they more often than not benefit from a variety of methods of communication and may also display idiosyncratic behaviours, due to difficulties in language development. Since most interactive partners will be unfamiliar with a specific person's preferred communication method(s) or the meaning of their idiosyncratic behaviours, repeated unsuccessful attempts to communicate or frequent communication breakdowns might lead to 'learned helplessness', which is characterized by low self-esteem, lack of motivation to initiate social interactions, and withdrawal and passivity, which McInnes and Treffry (1982: 9) call 'the total isolation of hypo-activity'. Moreover, given the vital role of both distance senses in providing information about the environment, it can be anticipated that more difficulties will emerge in relation to socialization. Children with MSI often miss out on vital information and perceive the environment in a way that is fragmented and not always coherent (Hodges and McLinden 2014). A child with MSI will face difficulties in accessing the social context and this makes it difficult for them for example to read social cues, learn age-appropriate social skills from observing and imitating others, and may also generate feelings of insecurity and vulnerability. Finally, lack of confidence to interact and to develop relationships may also be linked to the primary difficulties in independent mobility. Children with MSI may require help to move about especially in big and open spaces, and need to be specifically taught independence skills. Restricted mobility and independence may in turn impact on emotional, social and cognitive development (McInnes and Treffry 1982) and the child's ability and willingness to interact and develop relationships with others.

Again, it cannot be overemphasized that the secondary difficulties described above would not readily apply to all the children with MSI, because they depend on numerous factors (e.g. amount of residual vision and hearing, presence of additional disabilities, interventions employed) that influence the preferred method(s) of communication, the amount and quality of sensory input received, and the extent to which unaided mobility and exploration are possible. Consequently, the primary consequences of MSI may affect social and emotional development in different ways. For example, children with early onset or congenital and total deafblindness may progressively acquire passive communication patterns, i.e. they may become withdrawn into themselves and end up seldom initiating social exchanges. This may be responsible for the wide spectrum of challenging behaviours often observed in this population of children (see Kamenopoulou 2005). Some of these behaviours, especially repetitive and stereotypic behaviours, are also typically observed in blind children (Warren 1984) and thus seem to be closely associated with lack of vision. Moreover, literature on disability and development (V. Lewis 2003) suggests that such repetitive behaviours may cause stigma, therefore further inhibiting social interactions and relationships. Challenging behaviours however, may be less relevant to children with good residual vision or to those with acquired MSI.

Regardless of the differences in the ways in which children with MSI communicate, acquire information and move around, social interactions are most likely to challenge these children, because social and emotional development is challenged by lack of or limited hearing and vision. Moreover, 'when problems are discussed in other areas of development, such as socialization or interpersonal relations, they are often attributed to the primary deficits in communicative abilities' (Warren 1984: 222). It can thus be argued that MSI is likely to co-occur with difficulties of social and emotional development and that children and young people with MSI might face enormous difficulties in developing and maintaining social interactions and relationships, and in participating fully in school and society.

3.4 Useful theoretical perspectives

The link between MSI and difficulties in the social sphere has been explored in the past by various experts in the field, including practitioners and researchers, who have drawn on relevant theories of development as explanatory frameworks underpinning their work. In this section, I critically explore the literature in relation to some theoretical approaches that have provided useful insights, namely, attachment theory, *social learning* and *social deprivation* theories and *sociocultural* theory. It is noteworthy that one of the most prominent Northern experts on MSI, Professor van Dijk, has drawn on all these theories (Miller and Hodges 2005). Following this, I will focus on bioecological systems theory and propose it as a suitable theoretical framework for the conceptualization of difficulties in social development associated with MSI. According to this theory, social development, and any problems related to it, must be explored focusing on the interaction between various factors: primary and/or secondary; interpersonal and/or intrapersonal; biological and/or environmental.

As a framework guiding my analysis, I will use some of the most well-known models of disability that, in a nutshell, are frameworks for perceiving disability and its causes. I will refer to the two most widely discussed and conflicting models of disability – namely, the *medical* model and the *social* model. In a nutshell, the medical model views disability as the result of biological causes that lie within the person and that should be fixed in order for the person to fit in society (Kamenopoulou 2020). In contrast, the newer, and now commonly reflected in international discourses and agendas around disability inclusion, social model views disability as a social construction that could be removed by changing the barriers that exist in society, not the disabled person (Oliver 1990). I will refer to the World Health Organization's International Classification of Functioning (ICF) model, also referred to as *biopsychosocial* (WHO 2001) and the capability approach (Nussbaum 2011), both of which conceptualize disability as a dynamic process shaped by individual and environmental factors, including biological, psychological and social.

I will argue that in line with the most recent theoretical perspectives, in order to holistically explore the difficulties that people with MSI might face in interpersonal relationships and interactions, and overall emotional and social development, the focus of practitioners and researchers should be on the interaction between individual and environment, since the characteristics of both continuously interact and shape developmental outcomes. In other words, from a bioecological systems perspective and an understanding of disability in terms of capabilities and functionings in everyday life, the child with MSI is embedded within a series of nested systems that constantly evolve, and multiple factors within these systems influence development and participation.

3.4.1 Attachment theory and MSI

According to Bowlby's ethological theory (1991), attachment can be defined as the strong, affectional bond developed between individuals and significant people in their lives. This bond begins between the infant and the primary caregiver, and, if it is solid, it promotes survival through the generation of feelings of safety and competence throughout the different life stages. As I mentioned in Chapter 2, van Dijk and colleagues in the Netherlands drew on Bowlby (as well as others), and focused on the role of effective early interactions (see Janssen et al. 2003). For example, due to the dual sensory loss, the baby's signals are atypical and not easily recognizable by the caregiver. As a result, the natural development of early interaction, which is dependent upon the extent to which both caregiver and baby are capable of simultaneously adjusting their reactions in response to each other's expressions, is hindered to a great extent. The challenges in communicating and bonding with the caregiver, can hinder the establishment of a secure attachment (van Dijk and Nelson 1998).

An insecure attachment affects emotional development by generating anxiety and lack of confidence. Consequently, every new social experience might intimidate the child (McInnes and Treffry 1982), which can cause also behavioural problems, and may result in delayed social development, and difficulty in creating and maintaining interpersonal relationships.

This explanatory framework emphasizes the role of the dual sensory loss and the infant's 'atypical' signals. Moreover, it stresses the poor self-image of the child as a result of insecure bonding with the caregiver, and views problems in social inclusion as a consequence of lack of self-confidence and feelings of insecurity. Thus, attachment theory can provide a useful explanatory framework, but it can also reflect the medical model of disability, because it focuses on the infant's disabilities as the initial reason for unsuccessful early interactions. The medical model, also called 'defect' or 'within-child model' (Mittler 2000: 3) focuses on the disabled person and their weaknesses, which prevent them from 'fitting into' the social world. The core concept of the medical model is that the problem lies within the disabled person who should therefore be changed or appropriately cured in order to adjust to the social context (Llewellyn and Hogan 2000). Indeed, it could be argued that drawing on attachment theory in the context of MSI might lead to overemphasis on a single factor, namely, the infant's inability to engage in successful interactions, due to dual sensory loss, and the diminished self-esteem caused by the resulting insecure attachment. Accordingly, atypical behavioural patterns and unsuccessful social relationships can be perceived as the product of a problem that is mainly child-related, i.e. the vision and hearing impairments. Although it might seem obvious that MSI plays a vital role during early interactions, it should be stressed that the behaviour of the caregiver during these interactions plays an equally important part. Moreover, even though attachment theory maintains that the child continues to form bonds with significant others throughout his or her lifespan, it has been pointed out that the strong emphasis on the bond with the primary caregiver diminishes the importance of other significant relationships. Some theorists have criticized attachment theory in the past (e.g. Harris 1998) for neglecting the role of peers in shaping a child's development and pointing out that attachment theory fails to consider the impact of peer relations on development.

3.4.2 Social learning, deprivation theories and MSI

Bandura (1977) perceived *observation* and *imitation* during early interactions with caregivers as crucial for the acquisition of pro-social behaviours and skills. With vision and hearing, two major channels of information not fully functioning, experience of the world and its elements, including people and their behaviours, is limited. Past studies on MSI and learning style (see for example, Arnold and Leadley 1999; Hodges 2004) suggest that some children may use different learning strategies, relying mainly on their tactile sense and memory. Moreover, the skills of observation and imitation are affected (McInnes and Treffry 1982), and as a result, the ability to use incidental learning or learning naturally by picking up cues from the environment, including the acquisition of social skills, is significantly limited (Hodges and McLinden 2014). Accordingly, due to difficulty in observing and imitating others, children with MSI have limited opportunities to develop age-appropriate social skills and, in addition, they may not always know what behaviours are considered socially acceptable (Glidden Prickett and Rafalowski Welch 1998; Petroff 2001). To sum up, if we think in terms of Bandura's social model of learning, it is possible to suggest that children with MSI do not easily internalize social skills, because they do not readily imitate others. Moreover, they use different strategies for learning, for which they need additional time and repetitions in order to absorb and internalize knowledge (Hodges 2000). In other words, not only do children with MSI use different learning strategies, but they also require slower pace and repetitions during learning, which further challenges the acquisition of information from the social environment.

Sensory and social deprivation theories have been considered by some as the underlying reason for difficulties in social development (Nafstad 1991; van Dijk 1991). Given that one of the biggest challenges in MSI is the need for an effective means of communication, which must be understood and used by all interactive partners, it can be extremely difficult for a child with MSI to communicate their needs and to control their environment. When a person fails to get a message across and to make choices and/or express preferences, on the one hand, frustration and extreme stress are experienced, which may trigger tantrums. On the other hand, according to the *learned helplessness model*, a series of unsuccessful attempts to communicate may result in passivity and withdrawal, and thus the child may only engage in behaviours that are somehow rewarding, such as self-stimulation and self-harm (Kamenopoulou 2005). As a result, children with MSI may display behaviours that are not considered socially appropriate and that can be either introverted, extroverted or both, due to the lack of sensory and social stimulation that they experience, because of their primary difficulty in communicating and interacting with others. Some claim that even challenging behaviours that are displayed by some children (such as self-injurious behaviours) can be explained as a result of their need to produce and perceive some sensory input. Moss (1993) suggests that such behaviours can be viewed as a form of leisure, drawing parallels between repetitive behaviours and activities like extreme sports that are socially acceptable and are not regarded negatively. This is an interesting perspective, which proposes the idea that people with disabilities are different in many ways, but that being different should not have negative connotations. All people need stimulation as opposed to passivity and boredom, and this is also the case for children with MSI, except that they seem to have a greater need for stimuli, due to their restricted opportunities for meaningful social exchanges.

Both social learning and deprivation theories can be seen as reflecting a useful approach to understanding MSI and development, because they both emphasize the importance of the context as a source of social information and stimuli, and recognize the role of others in social interactions. In social learning theory, others play an important role as instructors of social skills through direct or indirect modelling. Although emphasis is placed on the different strategies and pace during learning of children with MSI, which might again lead to assumptions about their ability to learn how to behave in socially acceptable ways and to create and maintain relationships, this theory acknowledges, nevertheless, that others also play an influential role in this process and that if they modify their own behaviour, it is possible to teach children with MSI social skills. A reflection of the social model of disability (Oliver 1990) can therefore be seen in this theory, according to which, if barriers in the surrounding environment, including people, are addressed and if the context is tailored to the individual learning style of the child, then it is possible to overcome difficulties in social interactions and relationships. The same can be argued concerning sensory and social deprivation theory, according to which, if a person receives sufficient stimulation by others, there is no reason for them to engage in solitary activities, such as aggressiveness or self-injury in order to create self-stimulation. Providing appropriate and sufficient social stimuli can in turn enhance social skills and support the development of social interactions and relationships. Again, the central idea is not changing the child, but modifying aspects of the environment, such as the amount of social and sensory input that the child receives, hence this theory is also aligned with the social model of disability.

However, it can be argued that by focusing on the environment and the role of others, these two theoretical approaches alone fail to capture the multiplicity of factors that play a role in the social development of children with MSI. The social model was criticized early on 'for its neglect of impairment and specifically the implications of certain *physical* and *sensory* impairments' (Stalker 1998: 15, my emphasis), and theorists warned that 'some of the most profound problems experienced by people with certain impairments are difficult, if not impossible, to solve by social manipulation' (French 1993: 17). One of the most prominent disabled theorists and early advocates of the social model, Shakespeare (2010), also agrees with this criticism. Given that MSI is an extremely complex disability that creates various obstacles in all aspects of the individual's life, it would be rather simplistic to assume that the social context is the only factor impeding social and emotional development. Due to the complexity of MSI, the biological and psychological barriers cannot be overlooked and should also be taken into consideration.

3.4.3 Sociocultural theory and MSI

A theoretical approach that equally emphasizes the role of individual and social factors is Vygotsky's *sociocultural theory*, that I already discussed in Chapter 2. In the field of complex and multiple needs education, as well as MSI more specifically, the work of Vygotsky has been, and continues to be, very influential (Hodges 2004; Miller and Hodges 2005). The concepts of ZPD (Vygotsky 1978) and *scaffolding* (Bruner 1990) feature prominently in approaches towards the teaching of children with multiple needs (see for example, Bozic and Murdoch 1996). As I explained in Chapter 2, Vygotsky's theoretical framework can be encapsulated by three main tenets: 1) the view of development as a *process* and not a product, 2) the idea that this process takes place during social *interactions*, and 3) the focus on the need to understand the *tools* mediating this process. Cognitive development takes place as a result of social interaction, through the internalization of skills displayed by 'more competent partners' (Meadows 2004: 166).

During the process of internalization, the role of communicable systems is considered vital, because they are the tools through which social interaction takes place and so they underpin cognitive development. In the absence of an effective means of communication, the child's participation can be limited, unless adults make use of appropriate tools (e.g. objects) to scaffold and support interactions. This highlights the role that atypical biological characteristics can play and the importance of the adult's role during interactions, with obvious implications for the development of children with MSI. Many have applied this theory to MSI, including Meshcheryakov (1979), who, as I mentioned in Chapter 2, argued for the role of *joint activity* in cognitive development, McInnes and Treffry (1982), who stressed the role of the *intervenor* to interpret and structure the environment, where learning takes place, and van Dijk and Nelson (1998), who focused on the use of *co-action* by the teacher to help develop turn-taking skills (Miller and Hodges 2005).

Although directly related to the cognitive aspect of development, Vygotsky's theory is equally relevant to social and emotional development and it is a useful framework for exploring the difficulties in social interaction and relationships related with MSI. Vygotsky saw barriers to participation in social interactions as having a detrimental impact on development and maintained that such barriers can be both biological and social (Daniels 2001). Hence the strongest advantage of the Vygotskian approach is the simultaneous focus on both individual and contextual factors, thus in a way fusing psychology and sociology. However, there are certain limitations of this theoretical framework as the only explanatory model for the difficulties in development linked with MSI. Apart from the variety of interpretations of the theory that currently exist, the weakness of sociocultural theory is that, much like attachment theory, it runs the risk of overemphasizing the role of atypical child characteristics in early interactions with adults. Indeed, numerous studies underpinned by this theory (see Meadows 2004) have focused on parent–infant interactions, thus neglecting other features of social life, like peer interactions (Burman 2004). In other words, the multiplicity of factors influencing social interactions and relationships calls for a broader theoretical framework that can be applied to relations and interactions beyond the adult–child dyad.

3.4.4 Summary of useful theoretical approaches

The theoretical positions discussed in the previous sections provide useful frameworks for the exploration of social and emotional difficulties associated with MSI. However, as I noted, they all conceptualize development in a narrow way, placing emphasis on one side of the problem, be that either the child with MSI or the person(s) with whom social exchange takes place. Using as a conceptual framework for my discussion the medical and the social models of disability, I argued that elements from one of these models can be reflected on the above theories. I moreover argued that some aspects of these theories can be useful when conceptualizing difficulties in the area of social and emotional development in children with MSI, but they do not offer a holistic account of all factors that can be shaping development. Given the complexity and the uniqueness of MSI, it seems that a critically stronger approach would be to apply ideas deriving from more recent and holistic conceptualizations of disability as the result of interaction between various factors (both individual and contextual). An approach that reflects this understanding of disability is bioecological systems theory, which I critically discuss in the next section.

3.5 Bioecological systems theory

Bronfenbrenner (1979) proposed ecological systems theory (EST) of human development, perceiving the individual as embedded in nested systems and development as shaped by the complex interactions between the individual's characteristics and the range of systemic or contextual factors that continuously interact and influence developmental outcomes. Accordingly, development is shaped by the interactive processes between a person's characteristics and multiple environmental factors. Furthermore, development is defined as 'the person's evolving conception of the ecological environment, and his relation to it' (Bronfenbrenner 1979: 9), a view that stresses the role of the person's subjective interpretation of the systems, in which they are embedded. The main concepts of EST can be summarized as follows:

1. The first system is the *biosystem* of the child, whose individual characteristics, including abilities and disabilities, play a significant role in development.
2. The next systemic layer is the *microsystem*, formed by the immediate contexts, in which the child is embedded, such as family, school and community.
3. The *mesosystem* comprises interactions between members of the microsystems, such as for example communication and collaboration between teachers and parents.
4. The *exosystem* can be defined as influences from wider systems that are not directly related to the immediate microsystems, such as policy and legislation.
5. Finally, two more systemic layers are proposed, namely, the *macrosystem*, which concerns broader cultural and social effects, and the *chronosystem*, which describes changes in all systems and their members across time.

EST has been influential on research concerned with human development, although in its initial stage a lot of emphasis was placed on the microsystem, which generated a high number of studies on the family system that overemphasized environmental influences without adequately considering individual differences (Kamenopoulou 2016). To address this, Bronfenbrenner and colleagues revisited the theory more recently, and introduced the term 'bio-ecological' (Bronfenbrenner 2005: 3; Bronfenbrenner and Morris 2006), in order to stress the crucial role that the individual's characteristics play in shaping development and to shift the focus to both individual and environmental factors. They moreover summarized the most important ideas of bioecological systems theory (BST) – i.e. *process*, *person*, *context* and *time* – and the role of the interactions between them, therefore clearly arguing that development is a dynamic process that depends on a range of biological, psychological and ecological factors that evolve over time. In the next section, I discuss BST specifically in relation to MSI, in order to demonstrate its suitability as a theoretical framework guiding both practitioners and researchers in the field.

3.5.1 Bioecological systems theory and MSI

In recent years, BST has been gaining increasing popularity in the field of SEN/D studies (e.g. McLinden et al. 2016, 2017a, 2017b). In 2004, when I first embarked on my doctoral research on MSI, I found examples of its adoption as a conceptual framework for the organization of literature reviews on the outcomes of mainstream placement for children with special educational needs (Odom et al. 1996, 2004) and as the basis of a research design for a study exploring the education of students with a hearing impairment (Foster and DeCaro 1991). A conceptualization of MSI and development from a BST perspective was missing from the literature and research on MSI at the time. In my research that explored the social inclusion of young people with MSI in mainstream schools in the UK, I adopted BST as the theoretical framework (Kamenopoulou 2012). I have written about the benefits and challenges of using BST as the theoretical framework underpinning my research (Kamenopoulou 2016), and in this section I will briefly discuss the basic concepts of this theory in relation to research and literature on MSI and, where appropriate, other disabilities such as a single sensory impairment, in order to provide a conceptualization of social and emotional development and MSI from a BST perspective. It needs to be noted, however, that my intention is not to provide definitive explanations for how difficulties in social and emotional development occur, but to highlight the multiple systemic factors that can influence social interactions and relationships in the context of MSI.

If the child is perceived as a member of nested systems, the first system, which shapes development, is the family, and the first interactions are those with the primary caregiver. Due to the absence of language during these early interactions, both the caregiver(s) and the infant display social behaviours that involve the exchange of visual and auditory messages, for example eye contact, facial expressions, gestures and vocalizations (Webster and Roe 1998). The extent to which an infant with MSI is able to perceive and respond to such behaviours from the caregiver depends to a great extent on their amount of functioning vision and hearing and other characteristics, which can all be described as biosystem factors. However, according to the BST framework, interactions and relationships are 'two-directional' (Bronfenbrenner 1979: 22) and reciprocal, and therefore the success of early interactions will also depend upon the caregivers and their ability to interact with the infant via appropriate channels of communication. Hence it can be argued that both the 'direct effects of sensory impairment' and 'impaired communication from other people' (Pease 2000: 40) may hamper communication and interactions of infants with MSI. Literature on babies with single sensory impairment highlights the ways in which early social behaviours are different in the absence of vision or hearing respectively, but also that early interactions can still be successful if the caregivers are aware of these differences.

For example, in her pioneering work, Fraiberg (1977) studied congenitally blind babies interacting with their mothers and outlined the ways in which the absence of vision may impact on early social behaviours: blind babies did not make eye contact and thus came across as unresponsive. Moreover, in terms of facial expressions, vital for the establishment of rapport, the babies observed did not smile at their mother's face (as they could not see it), but they did smile in response to her voice, although infrequently and unpredictably, and they furthermore tended to display facial expressions that were difficult to recognize, which further confused the mother. Finally, blind babies tended to vocalize less and they were likely not to gesture towards specific people and/or objects, thus giving the impression that they were unmotivated and withdrawn. More importantly however, Fraiberg's observations showed that blind babies did convey messages, but that the mother had to look 'away from the face to discover them' (Fraiberg 1977: 102), because these were often expressed by signs and movements. Accordingly, in the same way that the baby uses a different code of communication, the mother/caregiver also needs to use different strategies to initiate and sustain interactions. For example, if they want to demonstrate affection, instead of smiling, they can employ auditory-based behaviours (e.g. voice intonation).

Similarly, early studies that examined the course of social and emotional development of deaf children from early infancy throughout the school years identified the differences in mother–infant interactions in the absence of hearing (Marschark 1993). For example, deaf babies cannot listen to their mother's voice, a powerful stimulus during early interactions. Moreover, the establishment of joint attention also becomes difficult, because deaf babies cannot attend to an object and listen to their mother talking at the same time (V. Lewis 2003). However, studies on the interactions between deaf parents and deaf babies suggest that these parents successfully apply a range of alternative strategies, such as use of touch, gestures and facial expressions (see for example, Jamieson 1995; Roos et al. 2016).

Accordingly, literature on vision and hearing impairment suggests that although significant, the obstacles placed by MSI during early interactions may be overcome if the caregiver employs strategies that make use of the baby's functioning channels of communication. However, infants with MSI cannot rely on either their hearing to compensate for their vision impairment or their vision to compensate for their hearing impairment (Meshcheryakov 1979). When the infant has impairment in both their vision and hearing, two important sources of information during early interactions are limited (or absent) and this also limits the possible compensatory strategies (e.g. touch, smell) that caregivers can use, thus making early interactions uniquely complex. In this sense, MSI places the baby and their caregiver at an extremely disadvantaged position during early interactions compared to babies with a single sensory loss and their caregiver. It is useful to remember though, as I stressed in Chapter 1, that the total absence of both vision and hearing is extremely rare in MSI, so the extent to which difficulties in early interactions will emerge depends on the amount of useful vision and hearing, as well as the caregiver's ability to use suitable strategies during early interactions (Pease 2000). For example, in relation to blindness, 'the child who has even minimal vision is more likely to show an interest in her environment, to make some visual contact with her parents, and may even reach and become mobile using visual cues. This may [...] make it easier for [the parents] to interact successfully with her' (V. Lewis 2003: 96). It needs to be borne in mind therefore that when some residual vision is present, early interactions might be easier for both the baby and her caregivers, and the same can be argued in relation to residual hearing, as the amount of available auditory input determines the extent to which the caregivers can use auditory-based strategies to establish interaction.

Apart from the role of the caregivers in using appropriate strategies during early interactions, from a bioecological systems perspective, other microsystem factors relating to the family should be considered. Parents of an infant with complex needs might experience considerable psychological stress, which is likely to result in frequent conflicts or even family breakdown. Moreover, the various responsibilities of caring for a deafblind family member are likely to have an impact on the siblings as well (Aitken 2000a). Consequently, families of children with MSI experience significant pressure as previous research has highlighted (Giangreco et al. 1991), which might contribute towards circumstances hindering development. Moreover, according to the BST framework, if dysfunctional behavioural patterns emerge during early interactions, they could be established and repeated during early interactions with the rest of the family members.

In summary, according to the BST approach, in the context of MSI, social and emotional development is the result of the continuous interaction between the child's unique biosystem characteristics (e.g. severity and type of dual sensory impairment, other disabilities, personality) and various systemic factors (e.g. the communicative partner's skills, family composition). In a relevant research article, where I reflect on using the bioecological framework for my research on MSI, I stressed that this theoretical perspective highlights 'the complexity and fragility of social interactions and relationships of these children, but also creates a framework for research, according to which these interactions and relationships can be perceived as reciprocal' (Kamenopoulou 2016: 519), thus equally depending on the child with MSI and a multiplicity of systemic factors. Moreover, this framework can be easily applied to any setting that can be viewed as a system, such as the family, school or community, and used to explore changes in development over time.

3.5.2 Benefits and challenges of bioecological systems theory

The main advantage of adopting bioecological systems theory is that any area of development can be assessed holistically, taking as a starting point the fact that the child as a separate biosystem has an influence on the other features within the systems, while at the same time being influenced by these systemic features. Moreover, the focus on the interaction between individual and environmental factors as the main force driving developmental outcomes is in line with the ICF model and the capability approach, both of which have been proposed as the most suitable and holistic frameworks for understanding disability (Mitra 2006). It must be stressed that the ICF model, adopted by the WHO in its most recent International Classification of Functioning (WHO 2001), is often also called the *biopsychosocial* model, but this must not be confused (as is often the case in the literature) with Waddell and Aylward's (2010) biopsychosocial model. For a criticism of the latter and a clear explanation of how it differs from the ICF model, see Shakespeare et al. (2017).

The ICF model's aim is 'to provide a coherent view of different perspectives of health from a biological, individual and social perspective' (WHO 2001: 20). Moreover, the ICF model proposes that disability is rooted in a health condition that causes activity limitations and participation restrictions that are continuously shaped by all the different contexts of an individual's daily life (Mitra 2006). Activity and participation domains can include learning and education and the contexts include many different factors, such as for example personal, community and cultural factors. According to this perspective, human development is continuously shaped by biological, ecological and psychological factors, with which an individual continuously interacts over time. The result of these interactions is the individual's dynamic and distinctive functioning profile. In other words, functioning and disability are the opposite sides of the same coin, with functioning representing 'body functions and structures, activities, and participation' and disability covering 'impairments, activity limitations, and participation restrictions' (Mitra 2006: 238). This allows for multiple levels of explanation of disability in terms of health conditions, restrictions in participation, and limitations in carrying out activities, and most importantly, the role of contextual factors is considered at every level (Shakespeare et al. 2017).

The concept of *functioning* is also central in Amartya Sen's capability approach (1985), alongside the concept of *capabilities*. Sen developed this approach in the context of welfare economics, and later on philosopher Martha Nussbaum argued that it could be applied to what she described as remaining social injustices, including justice for those with physical or mental impairment (Nussbaum 2004). However, it should be stressed that the notion of functioning in the capability approach is slightly different to the notion of functioning in the ICF model, because the former has a broader meaning that includes activities (what an individual can do) but also desirable states (what they desire to do) (Mitra 2006). In the same way, capabilities include abilities and skills, but also the potential to make the most out of them (Nussbaum 2011). To illustrate the difference between the meaning of capabilities and functionings, I will give an example: a child with MSI, who does not take part in playtime with peers during breaktime, because they prefer to read a book, differs from a child with MSI, who spends breaktime alone, because they experience intimidation and bullying. They both achieve the same functioning (spending breaktime alone), but they have very different capabilities (the first child *chose* to be alone because this is their preference, whereas the second child did not have the opportunity to choose, hence they are alone due to the specific social context). For a fuller discussion of the capability approach, its commonalities and differences from the ICF model, and the advantages of both models compared to some of the most well-known models of disability, see Mitra (2006). For a discussion arguing for the application of the capability approach to the education of children with S/PMLD, see Imray and Colley (2017).

To sum up, the common point between the ICF model and the capability approach is the emphasis on the role personal factors, such as impairment, as well as environmental and sociocultural influences, such as mental health, interpersonal relationships, and poverty. The bioecological systems theoretical approach reflects this perspective, as it calls for an exploration of 'multiple factors within and across systems thus rejecting the 'either/or' question concerning the degree to which outcomes depend on the individual or the context' (Kamenopoulou 2016: 523). It moreover can be argued that the conceptualization of MSI and development from a bioecological systems perspective includes elements of all the theories discussed in the previous sections, namely, attachment, social learning and deprivation theories, as well sociocultural theory. Furthermore, the perception of the contexts, in which the individual is embedded, as 'a nested arrangement of concentric structures, each contained within the next' (Bronfenbrenner 1979: 22) makes possible the consideration of wider systemic factors that are beyond the immediate microsystems, such as the role of influences from policy and legislation. Hence the bioecological systems theoretical framework can capture a multiplicity of factors that are either close to the child or part of contexts, in which the child does not directly participate, but do affect development. Moreover, as I stressed before, this theoretical approach helps capture the various interrelated systemic factors and their evolving interaction over time.

Finally, the main challenge associated with the adoption of bioecological systems theory is the number and complexity factors that must be explored for a holistic assessment of what influences development in each unique case, which can be a daunting prospect for both practitioners and researchers using this theoretical lens in their work. It is helpful, however, to emphasize that 'it is neither necessary nor possible to meet all the criteria for ecological research within a single investigation' (Bronfenbrenner 1979: 14). This means that in research, bioecological systems theory can be used flexibly to inform and underpin different types of research design (Bronfenbrenner and Morris 2006). In practice, it can underpin a holistic assessment of the multiplicity of factors that play an influential role in learning and the ways in which they interact and shape development.

3.6 Summary of impact on development and implications for education

To summarize the key points made in this chapter, regardless of the great heterogeneity of the population, it is commonly accepted that MSI primarily affects children's ability to gather information about their environment, to communicate and to move around independently. Secondary effects include difficulties in the area of social and emotional development, such as feelings of insecurity, lack of confidence and challenges in socializing, creating and maintaining friendships. The implications of these difficulties for learning are numerous and complex, and consequently, professionals need to employ specific strategies in order to successfully support children with MSI in education. These strategies might include explicit teaching and modelling of skills that typically developing children pick up naturally, such as strategies for gathering information about the environment and its elements, including *space* and *time*, communicating with others, developing orientation, mobility and turn-taking skills, and developing trust in relationships with others. In Chapter 4, I present and discuss in detail educational strategies and interventions that are beneficial for learners with MSI, but here I stress some key implications for education and some key principles that professionals should always take into consideration.

First, due to the heterogeneity of learners with MSI and the uniqueness of each individual case, it is very important for educators to keep an open mind and to avoid making any assumptions about a learner and what they can achieve just because they are deafblind. The starting point should always be a thorough assessment of each child's unique mix of abilities and strengths, as well as weaknesses and challenges, especially in relation to communication. An effective assessment is key when working with a learner with MSI, because it will support an educational plan that is tailored to this particular child's needs and strengths. I further discuss assessment in specific relation to communication in Chapter 4. Second, after a holistic assessment, a major priority is the development of *communication*, a key area affected by MSI, especially in early onset or congenital deafblindness, which is why it is usually the main focus in educational planning (and in research, as I demonstrated in Chapter 2). Supporting and developing communication is crucial, because it concerns all those interacting with a child in any setting, such as parents, siblings and friends. Teachers must feel confident and able to assess, support and further develop effective communication in learners with MSI, and this is challenging to achieve, given the lack of training and resources for professionals on MSI that I discussed in Chapter 1.

In the next chapter, which is focused on practice, I present and discuss appropriate strategies that professionals can use in order to maximize the cognitive, language, physical, social and emotional development of learners with MSI in any educational setting, including mainstream and special. General adaptations of the learning environment, teaching style and teaching materials are discussed, as well as some specialized strategies and resources designed to support practitioners in meeting the particular needs of learners with MSI.

4 Practice: educational strategies

4.1 MSI, educational implications, and areas of need

The relevant practitioner-oriented literature about MSI (see for example, McInnes and Treffry 1982; Aitken et al. 2000; Miller and Hodges 2005) contains numerous educational approaches and strategies, with a lot of overlap between them. For example, the need for repetitive experiences and extra time to process these experiences is a strategy that can be useful when applying a range of other strategies, such as the development of communication or the enhancement of orientation and mobility skills. I argue that it is helpful for professionals to know exactly how the various strategies available are linked to (and consequently support) the specific areas of need of learners with MSI, as well as the specific domains or skills that each strategy is designed to enhance. Thinking about the *areas of need* or the *educational implications* of MSI, can help link the various strategies to the specific areas of development that they support, and this is the approach that I have adopted in this chapter.

In order to categorize the plethora of strategies available according to the main areas of need of children with MSI to which they correspond, I looked at how others, including myself, have previously presented the different strategies. In a literature-based study that I conducted on teaching children with MSI (Kamenopoulou 2004), I identified the following strategies:

1. Supporting and developing communication
2. Maximizing sensory input (includes touch, hearing and vision)
3. Teaching style (time and repetitions, reactive, prompting, scaffolding)
4. Building memory and anticipation (routines, cognitive skills)
5. Mobility/independence (includes access to physical education)
6. Use of interactive technology
7. Social development

In a rapid evidence assessment of successful strategies for children with MSI, Hodges et al. (2019: 17) identified 13 educational strategies:

1. Communication
2. Literacy
3. Numeracy

4 Access to examinations
5 Mobility and independence
6 Cognitive skills
7 Emotional and social functioning
8 Use of technology
9 Vision and auditory training
10 Teaching support
11 Teaching strategies
12 Minority language
13 Inclusion

More than 20 years earlier, Porter et al. (1997) had conducted a study on strategies used in England for deafblind learners, and identified two major types: 1) pedagogic strategies, and 2) strategies relating to the organization of learning. Moreover, they found that the strategies most frequently used by teachers were: 1) objects of reference, 2) co-active movement, 3) hand over hand, 4) structured routines, and 5) smell cues. What is relevant to this discussion is that Porter et al. found that some strategies were employed to support the use of other strategies, and they called these 'meta-strategies' (see also Miller and McLarty 2000: 151). One example they mention is the use of music as a 'meta-strategy', often used to support other strategies such as the development of communication, the use of routines or co-active movement activities. Similarly, using an appropriate teaching style or approach could be argued to be a 'meta-strategy', because it underpins every teaching and learning activity.

In order to categorize and coherently present the different strategies for the purposes of this chapter, I used as a starting point the three main areas primarily affected by MSI: 1) communication, 2) independent mobility and orientation, and 3) access to information, as discussed in detail in Chapter 3, and I specifically considered their educational implications. Obstacles in both expressive and receptive communication will profoundly shape every interaction that might take place within the learning environment and they will affect the development of *language* and *communication* skills. Furthermore, successful or unsuccessful communication has the potential to influence the development of a range of other skills, e.g. *cognitive* and *socio-emotional* development. Communication is the main area affected by MSI and without the development of communication, no learning or socialization can take place, hence it can be argued that developing communication is the first 'meta-strategy' when working with children with MSI.

Similar to communication, I argue that another 'meta-strategy' is *access and independence*. Ensuring access to the environment requires various adaptations to materials, spaces and resources in order to meet the needs of children and young people with limited or no vision and hearing, and it also includes specific training in independent mobility and orientation skills. Access to examinations, teaching support and inclusion (Hodges et al. 2019) can be argued to fall under this generic category. Limited orientation and mobility skills shape *physical* development, which includes understanding one's own body in relation to the environment, including other people and objects (also called sense of proprioception), *fine* and *gross* motor sense of balance and how the body moves in space (also called vestibular sense), and ability to independently and confidently move about and explore the environment. Ensuring access requires *adapting* the environment to make it safe and accessible for all learners according to whole-school inclusive approaches, which arguably benefit everyone, but it also requires *structuring the environment* with the specific needs of learners with MSI in mind and providing them with strategies that enable them to navigate spaces and daily activities independently.

Limited or distorted information about the surrounding environment is the next major area of need in MSI, and if not supported, it will affect the development of *cognitive* skills, such as the ability to build a world knowledge, including understanding of time and space, cause and consequence, and the ability for abstract thought. Children with MSI have limited opportunities for incidental learning or learning naturally from observation and imitation (Hodges et al. 2019). Hence their teaching cannot be left to chance (McInnes and Treffry 1982; Murdoch 1997; Hodges and McLinden 2014), and consequently, *building world knowledge* is another strategy, which also includes maximizing sensory input or supporting the use of all available sensory channels. A third 'meta-strategy' related to this area of which I propose, and which affects and deeply shapes the entire learning experience, is the use of an appropriate *teaching style* or *approach*. Miller and McLarty (2000) present an array of teaching strategies that relate to the organization of learning, such as for example allowing *extra time* and ensuring *repetition* for the child to process new information, to explore and absorb knowledge about the surrounding environment or to respond to a cue.

The final area of need that I have identified is *social* and *emotional development*, which as I have explained in Chapter 3 is one of the secondary areas affected by MSI. To directly support social and emotional development in children with MSI, the teacher must focus on the creation and maintenance of interactions and relationships, with both adults and peers. Establishing a strong adult–child relationship is crucial in MSI, because the learner must feel safe and able to trust the adult working with him/her in order for learning to take place (Clark 2000). However, it is also crucial to support the child to participate in meaningful peer interactions and to establish friendships, because *nurturing peer relationships* will enhance *social skills development* and increase confidence and motivation.

In Table 4.1 I list the strategies as I have categorized them for the purposes of this chapter, mapped against the areas of need that they support or the educational implications that they are designed to address. In the last column, I indicate the specific developmental domains or skills that are enhanced by each of these strategies.

In the rest of the chapter, I present and discuss in detail these five strategies and their core elements. For this discussion, I draw for the most part on key practitioner-oriented literature, which might seem outdated, but has made significant and timeless contributions to the field of MSI, such as the work of McInnes and Treffry (1982), the van Dijk approach (e.g. Nelson et al. 2009), the

Table 4.1 Educational strategies for learners with MSI

Educational strategy	Details	Area of need supported	Abilities/domains enhanced
Communication	Includes assessment and development	Communication Meta-strategy (all areas)	Language and communication skills All other domains/skills
Access and independence	Includes adaptations, structuring environment, and mobility, orientation and life skills	Orientation and mobility Meta-strategy (all areas)	Physical skills (fine and gross motor skills, sensory awareness) Emotional skills (confidence and motivation) All other domains/skills
Teaching style/ approach	Includes extra time, repetitions, appropriate pace, prompting, scaffolding	Meta-strategy (all areas)	Cognitive skills All other domains/skills
Building world knowledge	Includes vision and auditory training or maximizing auditory and visual input	Acquiring information about the environment	Cognitive skills
Nurturing peer relationships	Includes creation and maintenance of interactions and relationships	Social-emotional needs	Social and emotional functioning and skills

seminal Aitken et al. (2000) book, and others who write about working with multiple and profound disabilities. Where relevant, I indicate the main source(s) that I draw on for the different sections, but this chapter is focused on practice and it is aimed at practitioners, for which reason I decided to keep the references to the literature at a minimum, in order to make the text more easily accessible to a wider audience.

Another final note to add here that the reader will find helpful to keep in mind, is that because of the heterogeneity of the population with MSI, some strategies will be more applicable to those children who are 'at the high end of the spectrum of ability', who are likely to use oral speech and be in mainstream schools, while other strategies will be more applicable to those children 'at the low end of the spectrum', who are likely to be placed in special schools, where they are taught

Table 4.2 Overview of strategy: 'developing communication'

Educational strategy	Details	Area of need supported	Abilities/domains enhanced
Communication	Includes assessment and development	Communication Meta-strategy (all areas)	Language and communication skills All other domains/skills

an adapted curriculum. Moreover, the applicability of a strategy will also depend on the type of MSI, e.g. congenital and total or acquired and partial, or MSI that changes over time such as the case of Usher syndrome. It is important for the readers to bear this in mind when reading this chapter, and to critically consider the relevance of different strategies depending on each individual case.

4.2 Educational strategies

4.2.1 Developing communication

As I have explained, communication is one of the main areas affected by MSI and, as a result, both expressive and receptive communication must be actively encouraged. This can be done by supporting and further developing any means of communication that a child may be using at different stages of their development. Unless the child is enabled to establish successful communication with others, they will not manage to progress academically or socially, and this is why I have described communication as a 'meta-strategy'. Van Dijk (1986) puts it eloquently: 'the establishment of communication and rapport is a prelude to progress in all educational and social areas' (cited by Sobsey and Wolf-Schein 1996: 440) Furthermore, communication is important, as it does not only concern the school environment, but all environments, in which the child meets others and interacts with them, such as the family and the community.

Here I present some communication methods that children with MSI may use, and some strategies that teachers and other professionals can use during interactions in order to help them communicate effectively. It is worth stressing again that the teacher will have to work on the establishment of a communication system 'from scratch' only in rare cases, and that more often than not the child comes to school with preferred communication method(s) or behaviours. The latter are what teachers and other professionals must respect, use as a starting point for assessment, and seek to actively support and further develop.

Communication assessment

For an effective assessment, in line with the bioecological systems framework that I discussed in the previous chapter and literature on deafblindness (Eyre

2000), every factor that plays an influential role in the process must be considered and this includes factors in the child (e.g. existing communication potential) and in the environment (e.g. resources available, type of task being performed). The aim should be to collect as much information as possible from various sources concerning the child as a learner and as an individual, and their behaviour in different contexts. Moreover, the assessment should not only be focused on the child's weaknesses (what they cannot do), but also, and perhaps more importantly, on their abilities and particular interests and strengths (what they can do). In relation to communication, this might include asking questions such as: does the child express needs and preferences and if so, how?; and does the child initiate communication or do they only respond to initiations? Other important considerations during assessment include remembering that all children communicate, although some children's communicative behaviours are not easily recognizable as such, developing a trusting relationship with the child prior to the assessment (it is not advisable for example that total strangers are involved in the assessment of deafblind children), giving enough time for the child to initiate and respond to initiations, and involving the parents (see Eyre 2000).

In terms of specific tools developed for the assessment of communication in children with MSI, I will mention here the two most relevant and most commonly used in practice. The first, the Callier-Azusa Scale 'H' (Stillman and Battle 1985), specifically developed for the assessment of communicative abilities of deafblind learners, divides communication into four sub-areas: receptive communication, intentional communication, symbolicity and reciprocity. The method of assessment using this tool is observation in a classroom setting, and the recommended observation period is two weeks. The second one, the Communication Matrix (Rowland 2013), which is available online and free for everyone to use, was developed for the assessment of the current communication level of people with complex communication needs, and provides a very useful basis for setting clear goals for improvement. This tool focuses on all types of communication, including alternative systems, such as Braille and picture-based systems, that are based on tangible symbols. It moreover includes seven levels of communication development, from reflexive or unintentional reactions through to the use of intentional symbolic systems (in the sections about presymbolic and symbolic communication that follow, I clearly explain the terms mentioned here).

It is crucial to emphasize that given the great heterogeneity of children with MSI, even assessment tools such as the ones I mentioned above, which have been standardized for the deafblind population, will not always be readily applicable or useful. Professionals therefore must be open-minded and flexible, and able to adapt existing tools or mix and match parts of different tools and bespoke methods, in order to tailor them to the specific learner, because no size fits all in the context of MSI. Moreover, communication level and skills are not static, and they continuously change and evolve over time. Finally, it is also important to triangulate sources of information by combining different approaches, including listening to the child and their parents, collecting data from observations and sharing this information with colleagues. In section 2.3,

I presented research providing evidence in support of all the above points, and in section 4.3, I further discuss these approaches.

Presymbolic communication (also non-symbolic)

A child who is at the early *presymbolic* level will communicate without using any symbols such as words, pictures or objects. They might use them in their communication, but not out of context, i.e. to represent concepts that are not present here and now. Hodges et al. (2019: 17) provide the following useful definition: 'Pre-symbolic refers to children and young people communicating through the use of direct, contextual means such as facial expression, vocalization or gesture, without the use of any referents such as objects, pictures, speech or sign.' Presymbolic communication can involve unintentional, spontaneous reactions or reflexes to environmental stimuli. Behaviours labelled as challenging or aggressive can also fall under this category, as they may be a reflexive way of responding to perceived threats and can consequently be seen as a non-formal communication method. Intentional responses to the environment that are presymbolic, such as pointing at a door, may or may not mean that a child is trying to get a message across (Pease 2000; Kamenopoulou 2005).

Cues are the next level up in terms of presymbolic communication but they are also partially intentional in their use. Cues are based on the association of places or objects with activities or individuals. Object cues can provide the scaffolding necessary to enable symbolic understanding to slowly emerge (Pease 2000). For instance, a bracelet or a scarf that a person is frequently wearing can help the child identify that person. Taking others to a place (e.g. the dining room) may express a need (e.g. hunger) and represent a request related to activities that usually happen in that place (e.g. eating). The importance of using cues was pointed out over 50 years ago by Freeman (1975), who argued that even the ones that cause a negative response by the child are useful, because they demonstrate that the child is capable of communicating their feelings, likes or dislikes by responding to cues.

Transition from presymbolic to symbolic communication

It is necessary to stress that when children with MSI are not at the symbolic level yet, they will exhibit individualized patterns of communication based on their unique profiles and experiences. For example, a cue that represents a concept for one child will not necessarily have the same meaning for another child. The use of non-formal methods of communication, such as cues or signs that are meaningful only to them, means that at this stage, they must be supported by interactive partners, who can interpret their communicative behaviours and ensure effective communication. Moreover, the aim of every interaction with the child should be the progressive development of a more formal, more commonly understood, and therefore more effective communication system.

The process of transforming the cues from idiosyncratic and unsystematic to specific and purposeful is slow and requires specific strategies. *Co-active movement* is an approach in which the aim is for the adult to enter the child's world (van Dijk and Nelson 1998). In the first stage, called *resonance*, the adult lets the child lead and simply reflects their movements back to them. In the next stage, called co-active movement, 'the educator follows and then joins in the movement of the child in order to encourage later turn-taking' (Miller and Hodges 2005: 46). According to this approach, formal communication is developed gradually when the adult helps the child develop an awareness of others, and tries to understand and successfully respond to the messages that the child may be conveying. Attribution of a certain meaning to the child's natural movements and initial vocalizations is the starting point, and in this way, the child's own experiences become the source of the communication cues. Consistent with the need to make the most of the child's existing repertoire is the key idea of 'joining in' the child's activity or focus, because the aim is to let the child lead in an activity or interaction that they find meaningful, and that takes place in their natural day to day environment. One example is to focus on one of the child's favourite objects (e.g. a pair of socks, a doll) in order to initiate interaction. As a result, the child learns that s/he can influence the environment and is motivated for further action and, more importantly, interaction (van Dijk and Nelson 1998).

By following this approach, the adult progressively transforms the unintentional, almost accidental and non-symbolic responses into intentional and increasingly more complicated systems of communication (Pease 2000). Consistency and repetition play a decisive role during the whole process (McInnes and Treffry 1982; Hodges 2000), because they make it easier for the child to build associations in relation to different cues, and to gradually internalize concepts, which are necessary for the development of a formal communication system. The latter can be easily recognized and interpreted by a considerable number of people, and allow effective communication in different interactional contexts and with different interactive partners.

Symbolic communication

Once some basic concepts have been acquired, the child is able to engage in meaningful interactions using symbols in isolation from the actual experience and in a variety of situations (Pease 2000). *Symbolic* communication systems are based on the use of objects representing activities that are not necessarily taking place at the same time as the interaction. Such objects may be real objects or representations, both visual, such as pictures and drawings, and tactile, such as tactile pictures, small objects or parts of them. This strategy, now widely used, is called 'objects of reference' (van Dijk and Nelson 1998: 3) and was first introduced by van Dijk and colleagues in order to help the child to take part in interactions, by making the concepts associated with them tangible and concrete. The more mature the child's thinking becomes, the more abstract the symbols used can be. When presenting objects of reference, good practices include: 1) presenting the same object every time, 2) presenting the object immediately before an item, place, person, event or activity, 3) using the object every time it is needed, 4) using the object it in the same manner every time, and 5) presenting the object with the same accompanying speech/signing every time (see Ockelford and Park 2002).

Sign systems

These are languages based on gestures and signals with their own vocabulary, grammar and syntax. There are different types of sign languages and each type may also vary from one individual to another according to their particular needs. For instance, the size of the signs has to be adapted to each person's particular abilities and, in some cases, the changes required are so great that they result in the development of idiosyncratic sign systems, which are unique to the individual using them. The most common types of sign languages used in the UK are: 1) British Sign Language (BSL), 2) Signed English (a 'hybrid' language created from the vocabulary of BSL, but the words are placed in the same order as in spoken language, 3) Sign Supported English (a language in which English is spoken together with some BSL signs), 4) Makaton (collection of signs rather than full language, used as a dialect of BSL, intended to be used alongside speech), and 5) Fingerspelling (signing technique, in which each sign corresponds to a different letter of the alphabet, not a whole word or sentence) (Pease 2000).

For the needs of people with MSI, all the above systems require tactile adaptations, especially in the case of severe and profound vision impairment (i.e. very little usable vision) or total blindness. For this to happen, physical proximity between the interactive partners is necessary so they can reach each other's hands, and express and receive messages through touch. Apart from the above sign systems, there is also the deafblind manual alphabet and a method that consists of tracing the letters of the Roman alphabet with one's index finger on the deafblind person's palm.

Oral speech

Although full mastery of spoken language cannot be expected from every child or young person with MSI, this does not mean that people interacting with them should not make use of this communication method. On the contrary, the importance of constantly providing the child with language input cannot be overemphasized. McInnes and Treffry (1982) encourage parents and teachers to talk to the child in the same way they would talk to a hearing and sighted child. In the case of children with sufficient useful vision, *lip-reading* can compensate for the hearing impairment and make oral speech accessible. Moreover, methods supporting speech perception have been developed and can be applied even in the case of children without much vision, and the Tadoma method is one such example. In this method the deafblind person places his/her thumb on the speaker's lips and the remaining fingers on the speaker's throat, and, in this way, the speech is perceived by the vibrations produced while the communication partner speaks (Dammeyer and Ask Larsen 2016).

Written word: print or tactile format

The main methods for accessing written word with limited or no vision are tactile and include Braille and Moon. The letters of the Braille code are made from combinations of dots that the reader feels with the fingers and interprets into words (Douglas and McLinden 2005). It is useful to highlight that Braille exists in different languages, hence knowledge of English Braille does not mean that the person can read Braille signs in Greek, when they travel to Greece. The Moon code is a simplified raised line version of the Roman print alphabet that is also perceived through touch (McCall and McLinden 2007). Finally, large print (i.e. print that is enlarged) is a simple method commonly used to enable access to written language for people with vision impairment, and it can be also useful for learners with MSI.

Aids

These are both human and mechanical. Human aids to communication (HACs) are intervenors, interpreters, lip-speakers, and other professionals, who are specifically trained to support effective communication with interactive partners not familiar with an individual's specific communication method(s), idiosyncratic communication system or behaviours. Moreover, a huge range of technological aids are now available, such as switch-activated devices that produce audio messages, voice software, video magnification of print and Braille displays. All these play a key role in supporting and allowing successful expressive and receptive communication, and I cover these in more detail in section 4.2.4. For an excellent discussion of strategies based on assistive technology, see Hodges et al. (2019: 94–9).

Developing a communication system: general observations

Most methods of communication used by deafblind people rely heavily on *touch*, which is not unexpected, given the absence of or impairment in both distance senses. Physical contact in this case is critical for the development of communication, because without anyone touching them, children with MSI at the presymbolic level may have the impression that they are alone and may become demotivated, passive and withdrawn. If they do not know for example that someone has entered the room, they are unlikely to initiate interaction with them. Physical contact is not necessary merely as an indicator of the presence of others, but also as a source of trust and safety. Methods such as massage and aromatherapy that are based on the association between touch and pleasant feelings can be effective in creating a safe and comforting environment, where contact can be established and a positive response can be encouraged (Pease 2000).

However, it is crucial to emphasize that some of the above methods of communication make use of the distance senses as well, with BSL being one indicative example. Such methods are appropriate for children who

Table 4.3 Activity: Developing communication

> Different approaches have been developed and are being widely used in practice specifically for supporting communication in people with complex needs, such as alternative and augmentative communication (AAC) systems and intensive interaction. Although popular among practitioners, the evidence on their effectiveness is inconclusive. In fact, we can learn a lot by reading studies on these interventions. In Table 4.4 I summarize evidence available on intensive interaction that I gathered after a scoping literature review. The following studies focus on the use of AAC systems:
>
> - Ganz, J.B., Simpson, R.L. and Corbin-Newsome, J. (2008). The impact of the Picture Exchange Communication System on requesting and speech development in pre-schoolers with autism spectrum disorders and similar characteristics, *Research in Autism Spectrum Disorders*, 2(1): 157–69.
> - Harding, C., Lindsay, G., O'Brien, A., Dipper, L. and Wright, J. (2011). Implementing AAC with children with profound and multiple learning disabilities: a study in rationale underpinning intervention. *The Journal of Research in Special Educational Needs*, 11(2), 120–9.
>
> Look at the evidence-based practice sheet on intensive interaction in Table 4.4 to gain an idea about what we know so far, the weaknesses of existing research and the gaps that I have identified as areas for future research.
>
> Next, read the above papers and any other research that you can find.
>
> - What are the benefits and disadvantages of these strategies, based on the evidence provided?
> - Can you think of any weaknesses of these research studies?
> - Can you think of any areas for future research?

have some usable vision and/or hearing, and those who acquire MSI later in life (Aitken 2000b). With or without tactile adaptations, these methods cannot be effectively used by those with congenital or total MSI, because they require at least one of the two distance senses in a relatively good condition, as well as a capacity for complex motor coordination (van Dijk and Nelson 1996). Consequently, the choice of communication method depends on the type of MSI – that is, the amount of residual vision and hearing, the age of onset and the simultaneous presence or not of additional disabilities.

To sum up, there is a wide range of possible communication methods for children with MSI, and their selection and use depends on the individual needs, level, and preferences of each child. Hence a bespoke intervention approach must be implemented based on a holistic assessment, in order to support better overall communication skills, which are critical to learning and to having quality of life.

Table 4.4 Evidence-based practice sheet

Approach: Intensive interaction

Overview: What it is, how it works and whom it is for

- An approach aiming to support the development of positive interactions between people with complex communication needs and others interacting with them, including professionals, family members and significant others.
- It focuses on the development of preverbal communication – for example, turn-taking, eye contact, understanding of facial expressions – and aims to make interaction an enjoyable experience for people with very limited communication skills.
- It is widely used with people with complex needs, including profound and multiple learning disabilities and autistic spectrum disorders.

Further reading:

Hewett, D. (ed.) (2018). *The Intensive Interaction Handbook*, 2nd edn. Sage Publications.
See also: www.intensiveinteraction.org

Evidence base:

- Popular among practitioners, increasing but small evidence base supporting it.
- In a UK survey of 55 Speech and Language Therapists, 85 per cent mentioned using it, but parent interviews showed it less well-known than practitioners claim (Goldbart and Caton 2010).
- A recent systematic review of research on its effectiveness identified 15 quantitative and 3 qualitative studies with 53 participants in total. 8/18 studies focused on children and/or young people with 25 participants in total (Hutchinson and Bodycoat 2015).
- All studies found some support for increased sociability and improved communication skills, but their methodological limitations do not allow any firm conclusions.
- Lack of rigorous methodologies due to difficulties in conducting research with heterogeneous populations with complex communication needs and the nature of intensive interaction, which is multifaceted and with components than cannot be separated from other factors (Argyropoulou and Papoudi 2012).
- Barriers: lack of time and support for staff (Kellett 2003). In relation to MSI, its reliance on visual, hearing cues and eye contact (Hodges et al. 2019).
- Enabling factors: team work and staff sharing challenging aspects of the practice (Barber 2008).

Areas for future research:

1. Quantitative and qualitative to draw on larger samples and more rigorous designs.
2. More qualitative evaluations, especially those focusing on children and parents' voices.
3. More studies on children and young people in educational settings.
4. More studies on the length of training and support needed for staff.
5. Studies that specifically focus on its use with children and young people with MSI.

Table 4.5 Overview of strategy: 'access and independence'

Educational strategy	Details	Area of need supported	Abilities/domains enhanced
Access and independence	Includes adaptations, structuring environment, and mobility, orientation and life skills	Orientation and mobility Meta-strategy (all areas)	Physical skills (fine and gross motor skills, sensory awareness) Emotional skills (confidence and motivation) All other domains/skills

4.2.2 Access and independence

Ensuring *access and independence* can also be described as a 'meta-strategy', because just like communication, if access is not ensured first, nothing else can take place, and greater independence supports participation in all activities. In relation to access, *structuring the environment* is an important strategy. Many existing school buildings, and other public spaces and environments have been designed for hearing and sighted people. Universal Design (UD) and Universal Design for Learning (UDL) help consider the needs of all learners, including those with MSI. UD concerns designing environments that are accessible to everyone, regardless of their ability or disability. UDL is a framework based on the design and delivery of flexible approaches to learning that can meet diverse needs (see Capp 2017). According to the UDL guidelines, the teacher must present materials and information to the students in many different ways, and provide them with multiple ways of engaging with the content and expressing what they have learned. This approach has clear implications for teaching methods, resources and assessment. By designing flexible approaches that respond to diversity, teachers can ensure that all children, including those with MSI, have full access to the school and classroom environment, learning materials and resources, and are taught with appropriate methods. In fact, it has been pointed out that 'the UDL framework's emphasis on engagement aligns well with much of the research on supporting learners with deafblindness, which has called on professionals to carefully consider the engagement, attunement, and self-regulation of the learner' (Hartmann and Weismer 2016: 464). Furthermore, the advantage of UD and UDL is that they are whole-school approaches – i.e. not specifically targeting a few learners, thus not singling them out for being different, but more importantly benefiting and improving the learning experience of every child in the school.

In terms of adapting the environment specifically for MSI needs, simply put, every element that is irrelevant and distracting should be removed, and every element that is relevant and helpful should be enhanced. The child must have access to as much information about their environment as possible and this can only be done if the latter is well-structured, consistent and easy to navigate.

For a child with MSI, it is easy to get confused or even lost in a place that is disorderly and constantly changing, because they already receive confusing or insufficient information about their environment. For them to be able to make sense of their environment, both the quantity and the quality of the stimuli received and information provided are crucial. It is important to consider all possible *obstacles* and risks, and always keep objects and furniture in the same place. In this way, the child is able to internalize the classroom and school space and to learn to navigate them safely and independently. *Landmarks*, that is, key points that can be accessed through different senses, indicate to the child where s/he is at and support orientation and independent mobility skills. For instance, changing the carpet of the classroom to wooden floor in the corridor could be one such landmark. Furthermore, labels (e.g. in Braille) for places, furniture and objects can contribute to a well organized classroom and school environment (see Hodges 2000).

Classrooms are very busy environments, full of lively children, whose body movements and voices cannot be easily controlled. It is essential to minimize all unnecessary background *noise*, and this can be achieved with the use of cloth, objects and materials. Carpets, wallpaper and curtains, for instance, absorb the noise produced during daily activities (Hodges 2000). Furthermore, an ideal visual environment has the right amount of lighting and is *clutter* and *glare* free. Surfaces and objects should be in colours that stand out and can be easily perceived by children with vision impairments. *Contrasting colours* (light and dark) help the child differentiate places and objects, and objects should be of the appropriate size (Hodges 2000). Last but not least, the seating position of the pupil plays a key role, because they should be able to touch, hear and see as many things as possible. Sitting close to the teacher or a peer or the place where a specific activity happens, can increase the quantity and quality of tactile, auditory and visual input.

In relation to auditing the environment, Exploring Access is a tool developed by the RNIB that provides excellent step-by-step guidance for professionals assessing how accessible their school environment is specifically to those students with vision impairment and complex needs, including MSI (Naish et al. 2003). In relation to *structuring the environment*, they list the following key considerations: 1) lighting and shade, 2) colour and contrast, 3) acoustics and auditory considerations, 4) obstacles and clutter, 5) changes in level, 6) signage, and 7) display. The result of such a thorough environmental audit will be the reduction of visual and auditory clutter in classrooms and other school areas, improved acoustics and lighting conditions that allow easier perception of sensory stimuli, safe and accessible indoor and outdoor school areas, clear and accessible displays, and signage and landmarks throughout the school that enable independent mobility and orientation.

Finally, in order to support children and young people with vision impairment and complex needs, including those with MSI to develop their independence, fully participate and take ownership of their lives, it is also important to focus on *habilitation*, which is, simply put, training in mobility, orientation and independent living skills (also called 'blindness skills' in Girma 2019). It is relevant to stress here the difference between the terms 'habilitation' and 'rehabilitation'. The latter focuses on people with acquired vision impairment (e.g. young adults or ageing populations) and aims to restore skills that have been lost or affected. The former focuses on the development of independence skills in children with no prior experience of these skills in order to prepare them for adulthood (Hayton and Dimitriou 2019). In education contexts, there is usually a specialist (called 'habilitation specialist' in the UK, 'mobility' and/or 'orientation teacher' in some other countries) working with the child in order to explicitly teach them techniques for orientation, mobility and independence. The work of the habilitation specialist has multiple foci and considers school, home and community. In the context of the school, the focus is on the use of sound, touch and other senses to understand and navigate the environment, the use of mobility aids or tools (e.g. long cane) to support independence, use of technology to ensure access and participation, access to physical exercise and extra-curricular activities. Habilitation specialists work closely with the child, family and professionals to provide training in mobility, orientation and living skills, such as dressing, cleaning or eating without support. The role of habilitation is also crucial when the child/young person is going through a transition – for example from primary to secondary school, and needs to learn how to navigate new and unfamiliar surroundings (see Hayton and Mort 2022).

At the Department of Psychology and Human Development, IOE, UCL, where I am based, we offer the only bespoke course in the UK for professionals wishing to become qualified habilitation specialists or assistants – namely, the Graduate Diploma in Habilitation and Disabilities of Sight. The course was one of the outcomes of the Mobility 21 project (2007–10) that was funded by the RNIB and the Department for Education to train professionals to become habilitation specialists, as specifically mentioned in the UNCRPD (2006): 'Parties shall promote the development of initial and continuing training for professionals and staff working in habilitation and rehabilitation services' (Article 23). The Mobility 21 project had three core elements: 1) a review of the existing evidence base at the time about what strategies work best, 2) the creation of National Standards for Habilitation, and 3) the design and delivery of an exemplar postgraduate training programme. The course adopts an educational approach based on child development, including psychology, and the emphasis is on the education sector rather than health or social care, as is often the case in other countries. According to the National Standards (Miller et al. 2011), under review at the time of writing when delivering habilitation training, effective strategies include: successful communication and close collaboration with the child/young person and their parents, initial and continuous assessment of the skills and needs of the child informed by a solid understanding of typical child development, consideration of any additional sensory, physical or leaning needs, environmental audits, including risk assessments, and training in risk management strategies.

4.2.3 Teaching style

The child with MSI will benefit from an appropriate teaching style or approach that supports their learning and development. It is important to remember that the child will need additional *time* to process information. For hearing and

Table 4.6 Activity: Exploring Access (1)

Step 1:	Audit different areas of your house (e.g. kitchen, bedroom, bathroom, study room) or school (e.g. playground, toilets, staff room, classroom) focusing on the needs of a child with MSI.
Step 2:	Record your findings, in relation to: 1) lighting and shade, 2) acoustics and auditory considerations.
Prompts:	Focus on textures and materials used for the floor and other surfaces, height of ceilings, artificial and natural light, position of objects, clutter and obstacles.
Step 3:	List any barriers identified and recommendations for changes to ensure access.

Table 4.7 Activity: Exploring Access (2)

Step 1:	Wear earplugs or noise-cancelling headphones and a blindfold or scarf (the latter is optional, as you can just close your eyes or switch off the lights if you do this in the night).
Step 2:	Choose and perform an activity that you perform on a daily basis, but that does not involve any risk. For example: • washing fruit or vegetables • eating dinner or preparing a sandwich • brushing teeth or washing face • getting dressed or undressed.

Questions for reflection:
1. How was your experience?
2. What enabled you to perform the activity with limited or no vision and hearing?
3. What challenges did you face?

sighted children, gathering information through their distance senses happens quickly and automatically, but using all senses at the same time while trying to compensate for limited or lack of vision and hearing is a time-consuming process. Manipulating objects or exploring places needs to be done slowly, and it is crucial to respect the child's *pace*, to allow extra time and to simply wait (Hodges 2000). For example, forcing objects into the child's hands unexpectedly (Chen et al. 2000) is likely to cause confusion or even frustration and to jeopardize the entire learning experience, which depends on the establishment of a trusting teacher–child relationship that creates a sense of security.

To gather the necessary information, the child needs not only additional time, but also *repetitive experiences*, especially when presented with visual and auditory input or when practising a new skill. For example, a typically developing child might not have difficulty in understanding and internalizing the meaning of new words, but the child with MSI cannot readily connect them

Table 4.8 Overview of strategy: 'teaching style'

Educational strategy	Details	Area of need supported	Abilities/domains enhanced
Teaching style/ approach	Includes extra time, repetitions, appropriate pace, prompting, scaffolding	Meta-strategy (all areas)	Cognitive skills All other domains/skills

to the context, in which they are used. Practising a new skill across different contexts and situations repeatedly will help the child master this skill (Hodges 2000). Therefore, it is important that the teacher provides opportunities for new skills and knowledge to be repeatedly used, reinforced, and solidified. A good strategy for achieving this is the use of a 'matrix skill' (Hodges 2000: 176), which shows how the child can practise the same skill in many different situations/curricular areas throughout their daily schedule, and enhances their ability to *generalize* and apply the new skills to other contexts.

The need for additional time, repetitions, and slower pace is tightly linked to the need to *break down* the learning process and tasks into small, manageable, and explicit steps. One such strategy is called 'task analysis' (Clark 2000: 103) and is highly effective, as it leads to the acquisition of learning goals in line with the child's existing level of ability. The teacher breaks down a routine or sequence of activities (e.g. preparing a sandwich) into smaller steps or goals (e.g. prepare the bread) and provides *scaffolding* by joining in the first step (e.g. help with preparing the bread). The scaffolding then gradually decreases as the child becomes more independent while completing the next steps in the sequence. The strategy of gradually decreasing the *scaffolding* provided by the adult is also called 'fading' (Hodges 2000: 179).

In terms of strategies that focus on the environment, as I already explained, a well-organized environment rich in stimuli of high quality and free from distractions enables exploration and promotes learning through the stimulation and simultaneous function of all senses. A well-structured learning environment is also essential for the accomplishment of another goal, which is the development of *anticipation*. Providing experiences of *stability* and *consistency* enhances *memory* and makes it possible for the child to predict the future and to learn to have expectations about future events. The sense of *security*, which is a precondition for learning to take place (Murdoch et al. 2009), is rooted in the child's ability to anticipate and there are many strategies for developing this ability, all of which are based either on repetition or on consistency, or both.

The establishment of *routines* is one strategy, and it can be achieved with the use of *calendars*, in which various objects of reference representing the child's daily activities at school are placed in a chronological order indicative of their daily schedule (Pease 2000; Murdoch et al. 2009). Calendars can take many forms, the commonest being a *box* or a *shelf*, where the objects are kept. Moreover, various aspects of the child's life can be organized in this way, not only everyday school activities, but also the days, weeks, and months (van Dijk and Nelson 1998). Calendars can help make the concept of *time* more concrete and easier for the child to grasp. Understanding the concept of time is a necessary prerequisite for the development of anticipation as a skill. Calendars can moreover support the development of communication, be a source of emotional security, and help teach other abstract concepts and vocabulary. Since calendars can be placed into the classroom or anywhere within the child's reach, they have no disadvantages. The only challenge, as I have explained previously, concerns choosing the right objects that are meaningful to each child.

If the chronological order of the child's daily schedule is always kept identical and all activities are carried out in the same repetitive manner, the child becomes accustomed to that sequence, learns when and how each activity takes place and develops the ability to have expectations about what happens next. To help the child move on to the next activity, the teacher can use *prompting* as a strategy in order to indicate the activity that is about to take place (e.g. a book to demonstrate the beginning of the literacy session) or *modelling* by carrying out the first steps of a task (e.g. reading), and then let the child complete the remaining steps by following the sequence that they already know well (Hodges 2000). It is useful to stress here that successful use of this strategy requires some training and experience, as *prompting* can easily turn into *leading* the child without encouraging his/her active participation in the learning process (van Dijk and Nelson 1998). Another risk is that the child may become too accustomed to the activities taking place routinely, and stop being challenged by the level of difficulty. This can be avoided by the frequent introduction of new elements to familiar activities, but only if the previous activities have been fully mastered.

Apart from objects, places can also be used as cues, indicative of certain activities. Accordingly, dividing the classroom and school into *areas* and *sub-areas*, each of which is always used for a certain activity, is another effective way of building anticipation. This strategy is based upon the fact that small spaces are more easily perceived, as the visual, auditory, and tactile cues are fewer, and it is easier for the child to memorize them. Thus, when the child is led to one of these sub-environments (e.g. gym), s/he can easily predict that the activity associated with this environment is about to take place (e.g. physical exercise). Finally, the child's environment does not only include objects and places, but also people, who should be presented to the child in the same structured way. An excellent idea is the attachment of identity cues to the teacher and the classmates. Nevertheless, one should not expect the child to immediately memorize the *personal identifiers* of all people with whom s/he interacts, as this can only be achieved gradually. Therefore, it is strongly suggested that at the very beginning only a limited number of people work with the child (McInnes and Treffry 1982; Murdoch 1997; Hodges 2000).

Table 4.9 Activity: Comparing MSI with single sensory impairment (SSI)

> Haben Girma is the first deafblind woman to graduate from Harvard Law and is now a disability rights lawyer and advocate. In her autobiographical book, she describes the experience of being deafblind:
>
> 'Sighted, hearing people can process multiple social details at a glance, details like facial expressions, body language, spoken words, and vocal inflection. For a Deafblind person, the world presents environmental information piece by piece. Each new piece of information has the potential to flip the feel of a situation.' (Girma 2019: 47)
>
> Questions for reflection:
> - How might teaching a child with MSI be different from teaching a child who has SSI (i.e. VI or HI)?
> - How might the environment influence the quality of this interaction?
> - What are some of the factors that the teacher needs to consider – for example, background noise/music, visual clutter/glare, poor light?
>
> **Further reading:**
> Girma, H. (2019). *Haben: The Deafblind Woman who Conquered Harvard Law.* Hachette UK.

4.2.4 Building world knowledge

MSI can lead to limited or distorted perception of the world, hence a priority is to help the child 'decode the environment' (Murdoch 1997: 362), and a good strategy for this is to help the child make the most of all their senses, including any functional vision and hearing they may have (Porter et al. 1997; Hodges 2000). Maximizing sensory input can be done in various ways, and here I discuss some strategies, focusing on touch, smell, taste, vision and hearing.

For a child with MSI, a lot of learning will take place through their sense of *touch* (Hodges et al. 2019), hence *haptic* strategies that focus on maximizing the use of touch such as regular opportunities to physically explore learning materials and objects, are essential. One such example is the use of books that have both print and Braille and/or tactile pictures or vibrating objects. Moreover, tactile teaching strategies (that are also communication strategies, as I have explained), include *hand-over-hand* and *hand-under-hand* guidance (Chen et al. 2000). Hand-over-hand guidance is when the teacher puts his/her hands over those of the child to assist for example in the exploration of an object or the signing of a word (Hodges 2000). The advantage of this strategy is that when a child is exploring a small object, they can directly touch it and therefore perceive it in more detail than if they were trying to perceive it through the hands of the adult. However, not all children have the same reaction to having their hands guided by another person, and some might strongly dislike the experience, which might also make them feel less empowered. This is the advantage of the now more commonly used hand-under-hand technique,

Table 4.10 Overview of strategy: 'building world knowledge'

Educational strategy	Details	Area of need supported	Abilities/domains enhanced
Building world knowledge	Includes vision and auditory training or maximizing auditory and visual input	Acquiring information about the environment	Cognitive skills

in which the adult places their hand under that of the child, and which allows the child the freedom to lead the tactile experience. In this strategy, the child can control the contact according to what feels most comfortable. It is important to note that all haptic strategies entail physical contact, hence require subtleness and discretion on the part of the adult to avoid causing any discomfort to the child (Aitken 2000b), and might also raise safeguarding concerns, which is a challenge, given the shortage of staff with training on MSI. Despite the challenges, developing the sense of touch is essential and should be a priority.

The use of *smell* and *taste* can also help enhance and complement the sensory information that the child receives (Hodges et al. 2019). These two senses are closely connected, because the ability to taste depends on the ability to smell. As discussed in Chapter 2, the use of aromatherapy massage has been found to increase shared attention behaviours in children with complex communication needs (Solomons 2005), and the use of fragrances on cue cards to help children with MSI make choices during meals has been found to be a promising strategy, although the cards used in this research were bespoke and it was difficult to replicate them (Murdoch et al. 2014). Programmes focusing on the stimulation of the senses of taste and smell in children with VI and MSI have reported promising results. Activities can be based on the use of herbs that have a distinct and strong smell, and can include planting and gardening herbs, cooking with one herb as the basic ingredient, making herb calendars and smelling maps for a school area, and the benefits for the children include enhancement of memory and sense of security, increased motivation and sociability (Tavoulari et al. 2013).

Strategies that make use of and maximize hearing and vision are also very important (Murdoch et al. 2009). These include training in the use of low vision aids (LVAs), such as video magnifiers, additional lenses and screen magnification software; and auditory training, with the use of hearing aids, or cochlear implants. They also include training in the use of vision and hearing together to successfully combine or integrate the information gathered through both distance senses. The majority of children with MSI will have some usable vision and/or hearing, so vision and auditory training is a crucial strategy. In relation to this, Hodges et al. (2019) stress the importance of listening to the child's personal preferences about the best sensory channels to use – for example, if they are more reliant on their vision or their hearing, regardless of how well each of these senses is functioning.

Being able to decode the environment through training in the use of all senses allows the child to make predictions regarding the various elements within that environment and enhances their cognitive, physical, and socio-emotional skills. However, apart from interpreting their environment, some children with MSI, especially those with congenital and total MSI, also need to be explicitly taught that they can *influence* their environment (McInnes and Treffry 1982). Derived from this idea is the strategy of creating a *reactive environment* – i.e. that is responsive, interactive and fun. This is often done with the creation of a multisensory environment (MSE) or *sensory room (SR)* (Hodges et al. 2019), which can be described as a space rich in 'visual, auditory, olfactory, tactile and kinaesthetic stimulation' (Pagliano 1999: 3), where the child becomes aware that s/he can make exciting things happen. The MSE/SR is usually set up in a separate room or a separate area in the classroom, where the child is given the opportunity to control their environment by using a wide range of technological equipment. A number of activities, especially designed by the teacher to meet the child's particular needs, contribute to the learning process, which takes place through interaction with a variety of specialized resources. The concept behind MSEs is that the child is not a passive receiver of stimuli, but an active participator in the learning process, because they have various opportunities to express choice and to affect their environment.

Many activities can take place in MSEs, such as what is considered the most effective method of teaching the concept of cause and effect with the application of *switch-operated systems* and *touchscreens* (Hirstwood and Smith 1996; Reed and Addis 1996; Murdoch et al. 2009). When using such systems, the child perceives the results of their actions immediately, and this helps them internalize the idea that they can make choices that have consequences. Because the latter happen quickly, these activities can be very beneficial for children with a short attention span without the risk of them losing interest or becoming passive. Furthermore, most of the knowledge acquired can be generalized and skills developed in the MSE can be transferred to other situations with the use of the same equipment. For example, when the operation of a particular kind of switch that controls the level of light is mastered by the child, there is no reason why that same skill cannot be transferred to other areas, such as the classroom or the child's home, provided that the necessary adaptations are in place. After a series of successful attempts to influence his/her surroundings, the child progressively feels more confident, and this is a major step towards the development of independence and autonomy. Apart from the instruction of certain skills, MSEs can also be used to teach curriculum subjects, such as history and geography. For example, a *dramatic representation* of a particular historical event can be easily made using the equipment available. Providing the child with many different stimuli makes the learning experience interesting and much more motivating and engaging.

In terms of the disadvantages of MSEs, it is often pointed out that their overuse can lead to the separation of the child from their peers (Bozic and Murdoch 1996). It needs to be stressed that using interactive technology does not necessarily mean isolating the child in a corner of the classroom or a special room,

Table 4.11 Activity: 'Hnd over hand' or 'hand under hand'?

Consider which of these two strategies would be more beneficial to use for the completion of the following tasks, and why:
1. Teaching how to zip up a coat
2. Teaching a new sign
3. Showing a tactile book
4. Teaching how to tie shoe laces
5. Teaching how to play the piano

but it can also provide an opportunity for high-quality interactional experiences (Hirstwood and Smith 1996). Another possible disadvantage is the risk that the child becomes used to the steps of the activities after several repetitions. Practising a skill (e.g. touching a screen) when it has been fully mastered and its result is well-known (e.g. the production of a sound), can result in lack of motivation and boredom. More directly related to MSI, is the risk of providing too much sensory input and this sensory clutter can create confusion. When a lot of equipment is available, it is tempting to use as much of it as possible, but it is useful to remember that it is also the quality of multisensory input that makes a difference, and right quantity means high quality.

To avoid the potential disadvantages of MSEs it is important that the teacher plans carefully, and that they are clear about the reasons for using technology. For instance, during the regular assessment of the child's progress, the degree of difficulty of the various activities can be continuously readjusted to maintain high levels of motivation (Reed and Addis 1996). The need for teacher training is also essential, because planning and delivering activities that require use of specialized equipment can be challenging (Buckley 2003). Finally, the teacher should ensure that the child's peers actively participate in different activities – for example, by initially helping the child press a switch.

4.2.5 Nurturing peer relationships

In this section, I draw for the most part on the findings of my doctoral research that focused on the social inclusion of four young people with MSI in mainstream schools in England, by exploring the quantity and quality of their peer interactions and relationships. I have published an overview of the research and its key findings (Kamenopoulou 2012) and a theoretical paper explaining how I used bioecological systems theory to conceptualize and capture the complex phenomenon of social inclusion (Kamenopoulou 2016). Here I focus on the key lessons learned about how practitioners can support peer interactions and relationships of learners with MSI in order to enhance their social and emotional development and skills.

In a nutshell, I found that all young people were experiencing some social inclusion, but I also identified several issues related to the amount and nature of their peer interactions and relationships, suggesting that they were not fully included socially. For example, I found that peer interactions were not always

Table 4.12 Overview of strategy: 'nurturing peer relationships'

Educational strategy	Details	Area of need supported	Abilities/domains enhanced
Nurturing peer relationships	Includes creation and maintenance of interactions and relationships	Social-emotional needs	Social and emotional functioning and skills

reciprocal, some evidence of bullying by peers, and lack of access to socialization in crowded and noisy school areas. Interestingly, when asked to think about the possible reasons for the lack of social inclusion, the teachers in my study mainly focused on the effects of MSI and its impact on communication, reflecting a medical model of viewing disability. Contrary to this approach, adopting the bioecological systems theory as a framework guiding the research allowed to explore multiple systemic factors, both in the young person and in their environment that interacted with each other, and as a result of these complex interactions, social inclusion was either facilitated or hindered.

Indeed, the research captured several facilitators and barriers that could be located within the environment (e.g. role of peers, organization of provision) not just within the individual with MSI. This has important implications for practice, because: 'several characteristics of either the individual or the context might hinder participation. Hence practitioners will find it useful to keep an open mind and make a full assessment of all potential barriers' (Kamenopoulou 2012: 141).

The first strategy is to include social and emotional development in the educational goals set for the child or young person, since the presence of MSI is bound to render social interactions and relationships challenging. In my study it was noteworthy that there were no targets related to social and emotional development in the young people's individual education plans (IEPs), even if serious concerns had been raised about a young person's social skills development and peer relationships. Writing about the English context, Miller et al. (2005) stress that the practice of setting IEP targets and assessing progress towards them seems to be 'patchy in all schools' (Miller et al. 2005: III), and they moreover observe that there tends to be an overemphasis on academic targets at the expense of social and emotional development and inclusion. The research literature also reflects this overemphasis on the academic outcomes of inclusion instead of its social benefits (Kamenopoulou 2012). If educational plans and research evaluating interventions are merely focused on academic targets and fail to consider social and emotional development, the latter will not be enhanced and in some cases, it is likely that they will even be hindered by academic interventions in place, as I explain next.

In relation to differentiation strategies designed to support the child during learning activities, such as one-to-one adult support during lessons, withdrawal for one-to-one sessions or the right to leave the lesson earlier to avoid crowded corridors, I found that they all had the potential to reduce socialization with peers. For example, one-to-one adult support and withdrawal for specialized sessions (e.g. orientation and mobility, Braille) is a necessary strategy, but it can have a negative impact on socialization. Balancing the amount of time spent learning away from the peer group with interventions specifically aimed at increasing peer interaction and socialization is essential. The same applies to adjustments such as the '5-minute pass', which essentially meant that the young person with MSI had the right to leave the lesson earlier to go to lunch to avoid having to negotiate busy and crowded corridors and spaces at breaktimes. This strategy again limits the time spent with peers doing the same activity and should be carefully planned. It is important to remember that individualized educational programmes are not incompatible with social participation, but they must be designed and implemented in a way that considers and equally fosters all aspects of development. Writing about accessible curricula for students with disabilities, Miller et al. (2005) describe cooperative learning and peer tutorials as 'evidence of a number of what are considered to be effective forms of intervention' (Miller et al. 2005: V). Furthermore, they stress that the employment of these teaching strategies is associated with positive outcomes in socialization and communication.

Specific interventions to actively encourage and increase opportunities for socialization with peers can include buddy systems or peer networks (Haring et al. 1995) and awareness raising among the peers about MSI. Informing the peers about the specific needs and characteristics of their classmate helps eliminate barriers to effective communication, as shown by previous studies on MSI (Downing and Eichinger 1990; Heller et al. 1995; DeCaluwe et al. 1999; Möller and Danermark 2007), HI (Jarvis et al. 2002), and VI (Arter et al. 1999; Buultjens et al. 2001). The young person's communicative preferences, abilities, as well as the difficulties associated with MSI can be explained to the peers in accessible ways, alongside simple training on strategies for effectively communicating and interacting with their peer. Adopting this approach is also likely to generate positive peer attitudes towards MSI, because 'a precondition for showing considerateness ... seems to involve knowledge about the other person's disability' (Möller and Danermark 2007: 54). To sum up, interventions that directly support social interactions and relationships, and therefore enhance social development can be aimed at increasing opportunities for socialization, eliminating barriers to communication, raising awareness and promoting positive attitudes towards MSI.

Furthermore, according to the findings of my study, practitioners must also be aware and ready to tackle another issue, the possibility that the young person will experience negative behaviours or *bullying* by their peers, and this was the case for one young person in my study. In this case, it was noteworthy that the teachers rejected the mother's account regarding bullying experienced by her son, although the latter was confirmed by my observations of his interactions with peers at lunchtimes. Hence an important lesson learned in relation to bullying is that teachers might not always be aware of it, especially because it tends to happen in the playground, when there is less adult supervision. Remembering that: 1) children and young people with disabilities in general and

Table 4.13 Activity: Streaming by ability as a practice

> - Below are a couple of extracts from interviews with two teachers talking about the groups in which two young people with MSI have been placed, following the practice of *streaming children by ability*. Both young people have been placed in low ability groups in mainstream schools.
> - Read the extracts and consider the advantages and disadvantages of this practice in terms of its impact on socialization.
>
> Teacher: *The group dynamic is not working and there are people in the group who are in there because of their behaviour not because of their ability, and they are very dominant, very domineering, very aggressive either physically or verbally or both, and there's a group there that do not get the chance to interact the way they should or work or learn, and (child with MSI) is in that group.*
>
> Teacher: *I can't speak of what she'd be like in a much larger group, but it is a wonderful small group and they do look out for each other. If (child with MSI) was in a group where we'd have, let's say three or four students with severe behavioural problems, then she would find that quite distressing, so in those situations she would not be as confident cause she wouldn't feel as safe.*

those with sensory impairments in particular are at high risk of bullying, and 2) that the latter tends to happen in large outdoor areas, is a good starting point. In addition, listening to the concerns of the parents (and the child) and taking them seriously will also help gain a holistic and accurate perspective.

Last but not least, it needs to be stressed that my study focused on mainstream schools and it could be argued that in a special school setting the social dynamics are different. This is because class sizes in special schools are small and have more adults present, which means that children have fewer options in terms of socialization and friendship creation. However, it is also useful to note that class groupings in a special school tend to be extremely heterogeneous. Children with MSI, who are at the low end of the spectrum (such as those with additional cognitive impairment or complex medical conditions causing other disabilities) are likely to be placed in special schools catering for a variety of complex needs not just MSI (Porter et al. 1997). I would argue that the small and heterogeneous classes in special schools resemble the class groups, in which the young people in my study had been placed in mainstream schools. The practice of streaming by ability had led to the young people being placed in low ability groups because of their disability. Low ability groups in the mainstream schools that I visited were small and heterogeneous, comprising children with a variety of different needs (e.g. ASD, behavioural needs, physical and sensory needs) thus resembling the social dynamic of a special school. For this reason, I propose that the considerations and strategies I discussed in this section could be relevant for teachers in special schools to consider as well.

4.3 General considerations

4.3.1 Listening to children and young people

The aim of this section is to stress the *need* for and *value* of listening to children and young people's voices and experiences in both research and practice. I start by discussing why we need to listen to children and the benefits of doing so, and then I present some effective *strategies* for including children with MSI and complex needs in research that I have found useful in my own work. The tips I share here, however, will also be relevant to practitioners, because research is influenced by practice and vice versa. In specific relation to listening to children, it is important to emphasize that 'much of the innovation around methodology for listening to voice in the early years stems from practice' (Wall and Robinson 2022: 4).

Article 12 of the UN Convention on the Rights of the Child (UNCRC) (UNICEF UK 1989: 4) states that it should be assured 'to the who is capable of forming his or her own views the right to express those views freely in all matters affecting the child'. The UNCRC is the most widely ratified treaty in history and it is useful to remember that it protects the rights of all children, including those with disabilities (Kamenopoulou 2018). Moreover, the adoption of the UN Convention on the Rights of Persons with Disabilities (UNCRPD 2006) reflects the social and human rights model of disability, which seeks to empower disabled people to self-advocate, because they have been historically marginalized and oppressed by society's assumptions about what they need and what they can or cannot do. Article 24 stresses 'the right of persons with disabilities to education' and the right to 'an inclusive education system at all levels and lifelong learning' (UNCRPD 2006: 16). Even more importantly, it recognizes that all disabled learners must be consulted. Many countries have ratified those treaties, which are now reflected in national policy and legislation around the world.

However, despite more than a decade of extensive international policy development, evidence suggests that children and young people are still not included in discussions about their education or other services they receive, and this applies to both research and service provision. In specific relation to people with complex needs, evidence suggests that the mechanisms established internationally to ensure that the agreed global education goals are met do not capture or consider their voices (Byrne 2019). For example, in England, the Special Educational Needs and Disabilities (SEND) Code of Practice (DfE and DHSC 2015) is the current compulsory guidance for local authorities, education providers and health organizations on delivering services to children with SEND aged 0 to 25 years. One of the key principles underpinning the guidance is the requirement for public agencies to support the participation of children with SEND (and their parents) in decision-making about the services they receive. There is growing recognition of the lack of children's involvement in the planning and implementation of inclusive education (Hodkinson 2019) and in a recent study on parents in England, who had a child with SEN/D, and were also on a low income, we found evidence that they and their children were not involved in the decision-making process (Kunwar Deer and Kamenopoulou 2022).

In specific relation to research and children with MSI, our scoping review of the literature in England during the period 2000–20 found that learners' voices have been underrepresented (Kamenopoulou et al. 2021). In the majority of studies conducted, we found that adults were the most popular source of data, and that when data from children and young people were sought, these were most frequently collected through direct observations, so the learners' voices were not included. It seems to be the case that researchers in this field traditionally choose to observe the learners participating in their studies rather than finding effective ways of listening to their voices and experiences. On the basis of this noteworthy finding, we argued that we urgently need more research focusing on learners' voices, as postulated in several current national and international policy frameworks. This is not to undermine the value of observing the learner that I discuss in section 4.3.2, but to stress that any information collected through observations should be triangulated with data from multiple sources, including the learner's perspective. When observation is used as the only source of information about a child or young person's needs, preferences, likes/dislikes, progress so far in relation to existing goals, etc., then there is a lot of room for mistakes and assumptions to be made, because the adult may impose their own understanding or interpretation of what they observe.

The value of listening to children and young people with MSI more specifically when working with them either in research or in practice cannot be overemphasized. As we have seen throughout this book, each person with MSI has a unique profile, and the way they experience their environment and its elements will be different in every case, depending on multiple factors (such as for example the type and severity of hearing and vision impairment or the presence or not of other disabilities, as well as environmental factors). Hence the first reason why we need to listen to the learner's voice is that the only way of knowing how a child or young person experiences a specific intervention or a learning environment, and what adaptations they think it needs to suit their needs, is to directly seek their opinion. The second reason is that feeling that they are respected and listened to is the basis for the establishment of a relationship of mutual trust, which as I have stressed, is a prerequisite for learning to take place. Last but not least, taking part in discussions and decisions that affect their learning empowers the child or young person, increases their self-confidence, self-advocacy skills, and ability to 'speak up' to actively shape their future, which as I have explained, is one of the areas that can be affected by MSI that is often associated with low self-esteem and a tendency for passivity and withdrawal.

In relation to seeking the views of children with severe and profound disabilities in research, the work of Ann Lewis is worth special mention, as she has developed methods for conducting interviews with children with learning difficulties (see for example, A. Lewis 2002, 2004, 2009, 2010, 2011). Here, I draw on this work and my own experience of involving young people with MSI in research (Kamenopoulou 2012) and I share some successful strategies. In order to enable the young people to share their experiences, I found that *semi-structured interviews* were the most suitable approach, because although they include a list of predetermined questions or topics to be discussed, they are flexible and can be adjusted on the day. Some degree of flexibility is very important in this case, because it gives the young person the opportunity to open up and share their experiences in their own words. It also allows the interviewer to make adaptations, when and where necessary according to the young person's needs, mode of communication, mood on the day, which would not be possible with the use of a structured tool like a questionnaire (Pease 2000). When the young person taking part in the interview has MSI, which affects the sensory input they receive and renders communication difficult, it is challenging to try and engage them in a conversation about topics they might find difficult to conceptualize and to talk about (Aitken and Millar 2004).

During the semi-structured interviews with the young people in my study, adults were present in all cases, apart from one interview, that was conducted one-to-one, upon the request of the young person. Adults with good knowledge of the young person helped resolve any communication breakdowns, by repeating questions (in a louder voice and facilitating lip-reading or in tactile sign language), rephrasing questions (breaking them down into simpler components) and prompting responses. For example, the mother of a young person played a critical role during the interview, as it turned out that the question: *If you are upset, what do you do?* was misunderstood by the young person, who thought that I was asking her if she was upset at the time of the interview, so she replied *'No, I am not upset'*. Her mother, however, reworded this by making it more specific: *'Tell her about when you have a fight with your little sister and you are upset'*.

Another important consideration when eliciting children's voices is the need to carefully plan how to approach sensitive topics. My particular study focused on the young people's social inclusion in their schools and I had to think carefully about the wording of the questions, so as not to make them feel singled out as different. For example, upon reflection, the question: *Do you have friends at school?* became: *Whom do you spend breaks with at school?* since it was a more sensitive way of eliciting the same information. Furthermore, it is necessary to

Table 4.14 Summary of tips for enabling children to share their views

1. Use semi-structured and flexible interviews
2. Adjust questions and questioning style to their level and communication method
3. Have an adult present, who knows the child well (to resolve communication issues)
4. Give plenty of time for them to answer
5. Careful phrasing of sensitive questions, e.g. about feelings, friends
6. Encourage 'don't know' responses/requests for clarification
7. Stress not knowing the events or views of the child
8. Use statements rather than questions
9. Avoid repeat questions
10. Avoid yes/no alternatives
11. Avoid successive prompts

remember the importance of giving extra time to children with MSI to respond to an initiation or to participate in a task, as I explained in previous sections, so this rule of thumb also applies when eliciting their voices. In Table 4.14, I summarize the tips for eliciting children's voices that I shared in this section, and I also include some additional tips from Anne Lewis's work that I found useful and incorporated in my approach.

Table 4.15 Activity: Involving children with complex needs in research

- Simmons and Watson (2014: 19) criticize authors for exploring the lives of children with PMLD by presenting them as 'objects of intervention and study, defined by the extent of their impairment and functioning'.
- Imray and Colley (2017) raise this issue too, and discuss the reasons why including the pupil voice is challenging in the case of profound and complex needs, e.g. difficulty with interpreting their voices or lack of researcher experience.
- Pearlman and Michaels (2014) conducted a study on eliciting the voices of children and young people with a learning disability (LD) during the EHCP process, in which they developed strategies for listening to the children and young people's voices and for exploring how adults around them interpret their communications.
- Read the Pearlman and Michaels research and consider applying some of these strategies when eliciting the views of children and young people with MSI. What challenges might you encounter and how could these be best overcome?
- Pearlman, S. and Michaels, D. (2019). Hearing the voice of children and young people with a learning disability during the Educational Health Care Plan (EHCP), *Support for Learning*, 34(2): 148–61.

4.3.2 The value of observation and reflective practice

As I mentioned in the previous section, in our recent scoping review (Kamenopoulou et al. 2021), we found that observation is a very popular method of gathering data in research on MSI. Observations of children and young people were part of the methodology used in 15 out of the 29 studies identified by our review. Although both research and practice need to do better in terms of including the learners' voices, as I argued in the previous section, it needs to be emphasized that observation is a very important tool in work on MSI, because it can provide valuable information about the child, their learning and progress, as well as the areas where they need more or less support. However, the use of observation is not as simple as it might seem, and a careful consideration is needed of *what* and *how* to observe, and *how to use* the information gathered (Aitken 2000b). The *what* will depend on the purpose of the observation – for example, if it is to establish the child's existing skills or to assess their progress during the execution of a new activity. In terms of the *how*,

Table 4.16 Activity: Developing and using an observation schedule for MSI

- Here I reflect on the key lessons I learned during the process of developing and using an observation schedule for my doctoral research (Kamenopoulou 2009).
- In what ways do you think that my reflections support the argument that flexibility is an essential component of observation practice?

Overview:

I conducted observations of peer interactions of young people with MSI that took place during breaktime with the purpose of triangulating data on their social inclusion gathered by other sources, including the teachers, parents and the young people. I conducted direct observations using the technique of 'event recording', i.e. recording each peer interaction that I observed during each observation period. Data collected through event recording allowed me to explore the number of peer interactions occurring, shown by the number of completed schedules. It moreover helped me explore their nature, by capturing some of their key elements, such as *mutuality, duration* and *purpose*. I also collected qualitative contextual information (e.g. place, peer interacting, and adults present), in order to tease out possible systemic factors positively or negatively affecting peer interactions. To record the data, I used a printed observation schedule that I developed from scratch, and a voice recorder (as a supplementary tool for keeping additional notes that could not always be recorded by hand).

Initially, I had decided to conduct qualitative observations in order to explore different aspects of the behaviour being observed. After piloting the instrument that I initially created, it became evident that a semi-structured format would be more appropriate to use, because the tool used for the pilot required keeping detailed notes, which was time-consuming and reduced my attention and efficiency as an observer. Moreover, a more structured observation schedule would produce data susceptible to quantitative forms of analysis, and this would provide a systematic and rigorous framework, in which to embed the rich qualitative data.

The semi-structured schedule that I created had only one section at the end for any qualitative aspects of the interaction that had not been captured by the rest of the sections. Hence it was easier to use because it allowed me to record data rapidly, by ticking the relevant predetermined categories instead of taking down lengthy notes. I moreover captured additional descriptions of the context of the interaction and of what exactly had happened using either the voice recorder or the 'comments section' of the schedule.

(Continued)

Table 4.16 Continued

> When conducting the observations, similarly to the pilot, in order to be able to record their interactions, I had to keep myself at a short distance from the young people. This had been easy during the pilot, as the child who took part did not move around a lot thus allowing me to closely observe all her interactions. All participants for the main study, however, were much more independent and spent breaks moving around from one school area to another and interacting with different peers. This made observations more challenging and for some interactions I could not complete all sections of the observation schedule. However, similar, to the pilot, I used a voice recorder to make comments about the characteristics of the interaction, if necessary. These were then transcribed and added to the last section of the schedule or used to fill in any of the sections left uncompleted during the observation. In this way, the qualitative comments helped minimize observer errors, which was particularly important, because I was the only observer.
>
> To conclude this section, the main lessons I learned about observations are that *testing* an observation tool is an essential part of the process of developing it, because it helps ensure that it is methodologically appropriate and practically easy to use. *Qualitative* observation tools can be useful, but also very *challenging* and *time consuming*, whereas *structured* observation tools are more *straightforward* to use, but take considerably more time and effort to be designed. Finally, the success of the observations will also depend on *who* and *what* is being observed and *where*. In a nutshell, flexibility, adaptability and open mindedness are essential characteristics of good observation practice.

there are various methods of recording observations, ranging from completely unstructured (e.g. diary with qualitative field notes) to semi-structured (e.g. reflective log) and structured (e.g. quantitative observation checklist). Professionals must find the method that is the most suitable, but also the most practical, because for example keeping qualitative notes can be time-consuming but this may become less of an issue as one becomes more experienced. Moreover, it is crucial to always cross-check one's understanding of the observed behaviours with that of others, including colleagues and parents. Therefore, in terms of how to use the information collected, sharing observations with others is crucial, as is being flexible and open to changing our assumptions for example about what a child can do, based on our observations and those of others. Working with children with MSI requires practitioners to be able to combine multiple strategies and to use the evidence gathered to reflect on and improve their practice (Hodges et al. 2019). As I have stressed previously, children with MSI are an extremely heterogeneous group, hence professionals will need to use a combination of different strategies or to mix smaller elements of different strategies, and to be flexible, open minded, and able to completely change a strategy if it is not working.

4.3.3 Brief note about the curriculum

Before I conclude this chapter, it is necessary to add a few thoughts about the curriculum, which will be particularly relevant to those working in contexts where there is a requirement to follow a rigid curriculum with little room for flexibility. As I have shown throughout this chapter, children with MSI will need tailored pedagogical strategies, such as the 'hand-under-hand' technique, but also specialized curricular areas, such as mobility and orientation skills. In relation to pedagogy and curriculum for MSI, Miller and Hodges (2005: 49) argue that 'without an understanding on the part of educators of sensory function and the impact of its loss, access to an appropriate curriculum and pedagogy is unlikely to be achieved.' They moreover stress that 'the area of sensory function has always been a neglected aspect of teacher education. Usually seen within the context of medical study rather than pedagogy, sensory function is perceived as being on the periphery of teaching and learning.' It is therefore important that the training of teachers and other professionals focuses on child development, including the role of sensory function in learning, so that they can better understand and respond to the needs of all children, including those with MSI. Some children with MSI will be at the high end of the spectrum of ability, and they will be able to follow the same curriculum as their peers, but adaptations and additional curricular areas will be required in all cases, and it is important that the teachers are confident and that they have the skills and knowledge necessary.

Those learners at the lowest end of the spectrum, who may have additional disabilities and delayed cognitive development, as well as those who are congenitally and severely deafblind will always need access to specialized or adapted curricula. A good example of a curriculum specifically developed for children with MSI is the Whitefield School Curriculum, a bespoke personalized curriculum with reference to the national curriculum for England, so that all students can benefit from learning that is tailored to their specific needs, underpinned by direct experience of objects, people and activities that are accessible. Specific aims include the development of skills in sensory exploration, information gathering, communication, interaction and physical control (Lawson et al. 2015). Another example worth mentioning here is the curriculum developed by the MSI Unit at the Victoria School in Birmingham that focuses on strategies for maximizing vision and hearing and enhancing agency, use of routines and stable experiences, among other strategies presented in this chapter (Murdoch et al. 2009).

4.4 Illustrative case studies

In this last section, I provide case studies of young people with MSI and questions for reflection, to give readers an opportunity to consider some of the key points made in this chapter regarding appropriate strategies for supporting cognitive, language, physical, social and emotional development, and how they could be applied to their own professional context.

4.4.1 Case study 1: Aisha

Background

Aisha is 13 years old and attends a mainstream secondary school in England. Her vision impairment was noted when she was a few weeks old. At the age of 4, she was referred by her school for assessment due to concerns about her general academic progress and she was diagnosed as having bilateral congenital endothelial dystrophy.[1] Her hearing impairment is believed to have been congenital as well, but it is unclear when it was first diagnosed. She has a moderate loss on the right ear and her hearing is constantly being monitored. She wears glasses and a hearing aid, and communicates using oral speech. She is verbally fluent in her mother tongue, Urdu, and English is her second language. Aisha attended a special school until the age of 12, when she was moved to the mainstream school she is currently attending, in order to be in the same school as her older brother, who also has a vision impairment. The other reason why mainstream placement was considered necessary was that in the special school, Aisha lacked interaction with peers and she had more contact with adults.

Current school and organization of provision

The school that Aisha attends is a mixed secondary community school, catering for ages 11 to 16 and with a total of 1113 pupils enrolled, of whom 45 (3.8 per cent) are registered as having SEN/D. This number of pupils with SEN/D is slightly above the national average (at the time of writing) and the same applies to the high number of students from ethnic minorities, and students with English as their second language. The school has a resource base, supporting approximately 25 students with physical and sensory needs, and Aisha is one of them. She is in Year 7 and joins her form group for all lessons, but always accompanied by a teaching assistant (TA). Special strategies to ensure that she can have access to lesson-related materials include seating at the front of the classroom, having all worksheets enlarged, in bold and with good contrast, desktop copies of all boardwork, and using a magnifier. She has a lift pass and participates in modified PE. Moreover, she has additional time to complete tasks and the teachers simplify instructions for her and break them down into smaller 'chunks.' Her IEP includes the following specific targets: 1) developing independence skills, for which she receives mobility instruction once per week with a qualified mobility tutor, and 2) developing keyboard skills, for which she has one-to-one sessions with the qualified teacher for the visually impaired (QTVI). Finally, no specific targets relating to social relationships have been set in her IEP.

---

[1] Congenital hereditary endothelial dystrophy (CHED) is a corneal dystrophy characterized by diffuse bilateral corneal clouding resulting in impaired vision.

Activity: Questions for reflection

1. What are Aisha's needs in relation to communication, learning and independent mobility?
2. Can you think of additional adjustments/interventions to support Aisha's academic progress?
3. What are Aisha's needs in relation to social development and socialization?
4. Can you think of any interventions to support Aisha's peer interactions and relationships?

4.4.2 Case study 2: Adel

Background

Adel is 14 years old, and was born with serious health problems, for which no clear medical diagnosis has ever been provided. He had gastroenteritis at the age of 4 weeks, which caused severe dehydration, and at the age of 4 months he had 80 per cent of his bowel removed. The mother claims that the doctors failed to detect the problem early enough and as a result Adel spent the first months of his life in constant pain, while she was unable to comfort him. He is registered as partially sighted, although his usable vision depends 'on the day'. The vision impairment was present from birth, but diagnosed at the age of 8 months, for which he had glasses prescribed. It is unknown when the hearing impairment emerged, but it was first diagnosed at the age of 2 years. He has been diagnosed with 'maximal conductive loss on the right, secondary to chronic suppurative otitis media' (doctor's report) and has had several operations for grommets to be fitted to both his ears. He communicates through oral speech, but at the same time relies on lip-reading. Before being enrolled in the mainstream school he attends, Adel spent 11 years in a special school. According to his mother, 'their input into his life was considerable', which is why she was initially reluctant to opt for a mainstream secondary school, but she was finally persuaded by the teachers of the special school, who argued that further stay in the special setting would delay Adel's academic progress. After having visited the new school, met the teachers and been assured that arrangements would be put in place to accommodate for Adel's health issues, she gave her consent for mainstream placement.

Current school and organization of provision

Adel is in Year 8 of a mainstream comprehensive school with 1514 pupils enrolled. The school has a high percentage of pupils registered as having SEN/D, and a resource base supporting 32 pupils with physical and sensory needs. Adel is also supported by the base, and special arrangements to cater for his health needs include a toilet and a lift pass. Strategies to facilitate access during sessions with his mainstream form group include the use of enlarged text, seating close to the board, and receiving instructions broken down into small parts. One of his main IEP targets is to develop his independence, in the light of his medical condition, thus he has one-to-one sessions with the SEN teacher twice a week. In addition, he is described as hyperactive, for which daily medication is administered to him by the school staff. In relation to his social relationships, it is mentioned in his statutory assessment that he 'needs to develop age-appropriate social behaviours' and that he 'can appear to dominate other children'. He has had sessions for anger management at home to control his occasional tantrums, but his mother claims that it has not been totally successful. However, no specific targets relating to social development have been set in Adel's IEP.

Activity: Questions for reflection

1 What are Adel's needs in relation to communication, learning and independent mobility?
2 Can you think of additional adjustments/interventions to support Adel's academic progress?
3 What are Adel's needs in relation to social development and socialization?
4 Can you think of any interventions to support Adel's peer interactions and relationships?

4.4.3 Case study 3: Frank

Background

Frank is 14 years old, and has albinism with associated nystagmus.[2] Due to the albinism, which was diagnosed when he was born, there is lack of pigmentation in the eyes resulting in reduced visual acuity, and he wore glasses at the age of 6 months. The hearing loss was present from birth, but the actual diagnosis took place at the age of 3 years. He has a profound hearing loss in the left ear and a milder loss in his right ear, for which he wears hearing aids. He uses oral speech to communicate, but also relies on lip-reading, and he has had intensive speech therapy since he was 4 years old. Frank has always been enrolled in mainstream schools since infant school. Before he went to secondary, at the age of 8, the family moved houses so the comprehensive school he went to was not a local one, but it was thought preferable because of its resource base supporting pupils with disabilities. According to Frank's parents, the fact that his school was far from their house was a setback socially. Moreover, there were initial concerns about his socialization, because he would miss out on conversations and some group sessions were difficult for him to follow. Interestingly, music helped him socialize: he joined the orchestra and attended music lessons, and during these sessions he mixed with other children. His school was supportive

---

[2]Nystagmus is a condition where the eyes oscillate and may increase with tiredness/stress. The faster the eyes move, the worse the vision becomes, and most people with nystagmus experience a degree of blurring. This is in addition to the underlying visual impairment caused by albinism.

of his music ability, and in this way, music soon became part of his school life not only academically, but also socially.

Current school and organization of provision

At the age of 13, Frank was admitted to a specialist school for music, where he is currently enrolled. The school caters for ages 8 to 18 and has approximately 280 pupils. Frank is supported by the SEN/D Coordinator (SEN/DCO) and a QTVI, and he has two one-to-one hourly sessions per week with the qualified teacher for the hearing impaired (QTHI), directly supporting him in science and working on enriching his vocabulary. He also attends a one-to-one hourly session per week with a TA as a backup for core subjects, such as English. For all other lessons, he joins his mainstream group without adult support. Teachers use dark pens for the whiteboard and provide enlarged classroom materials. They moreover indicate who speaks during discussion time, so that Frank knows whose lips to read. To foster socialization, the teachers designed and developed a buddy system in the class since he first joined the school, which plays a decisive role in him becoming socially included in the peer group.

Activity: Questions for reflection

1. What are Frank's needs in relation to communication, learning and independent mobility?
2. Can you think of additional adjustments/interventions to support Frank's academic progress?
3. What are Frank's needs in relation to social development and socialization?
4. Can you think of any interventions to support Frank's peer interactions and relationships?

4.4.4 Case study 4: Elena

Background

Elena is 17 years old, and she has a congenital and deteriorative dual sensory loss, as a result of rubella. She was born with cataracts and, at the age of 3 months, had one eye operated on. Soon afterwards she had the other eye operated on, but the operation for the second eye was not successful and had to be repeated, again without success. Even though she only used one eye, she had quite good vision as a child, but at the age of 13 her vision started to deteriorate, and she is now registered as blind, following a diagnosis that took place when she was 16. However, she is still wearing glasses, 'for emotional reasons', as her parents and teacher put it. The hearing loss is profound and it was diagnosed at the age of 9, for which she wore hearing aids. At the age of 16, she had a cochlear implant and will soon have another one for the other ear, but she still uses the hearing aids. Elena communicates using oral speech. Attempts of the teacher to introduce her to Braille have repeatedly failed, as Elena's tactile sense is not yet sufficiently developed.

Current school and organization of provision

Elena lives in a rural area, and she has always been enrolled in her mainstream local school, where she is the only disabled student. When her vision started to deteriorate, at the age of 13, she was placed in an 'inclusion unit', where students with learning difficulties spend some hours per week, taught the main subjects in a simplified way. The variety of different needs within this context (e.g. dyslexia, ADHD) meant that Elena's very specific multisensory needs could not be fully met. It soon became clear that Elena needed other types of support and an SEN teacher was requested and, subsequently, allocated to her. Initially, the SEN teacher accompanied Elena during all lessons, but due to her profound hearing loss, support could not be provided effectively. The teacher therefore started to withdraw Elena for three to four one-to-one hourly sessions per day for the subject of English. She joins her mainstream class in order to socialize and this is the main reason why she was not placed in a special school when her vision started to significantly challenge her everyday school interactions.

Activity: Questions for reflection

1 What are Elena's needs in relation to communication, learning and independent mobility?
2 Can you think of additional adjustments/interventions to support Elena's academic progress?
3 What are Elena's needs in relation to social development and socialization?
4 Can you think of any interventions to support Elena's peer interactions and relationships?

4.5 Summary

As I have shown in this chapter, despite the huge impact that MSI can have on various areas of development, there are numerous strategies that teachers can apply in order to maximize the academic and social outcomes of such pupils, in both special and mainstream education settings. It is crucial to stress that possible interventions may vary from the simplest adaptations to the use of cutting-edge accessibility devices. Moreover, some can be described as generally helpful, that is, for the teaching of all children and/or of those with a single sensory impairment, while there are also specialized strategies for learners with MSI, which are designed to address their specific needs. Given that pupils with MSI are at a disadvantaged position as far as incidental learning is concerned, their teaching cannot be left to chance, but must be thought through and planned meticulously, as well as continuously evaluated and adjusted if necessary. Since different strategies are likely to support the learning process, although in different degrees, they should be considered as equally important and they must therefore be part of every teacher's repertoire.

5 Future directions in research, theory and practice

5.1 Research: what do we need to explore better or more?

In Chapter 2, I reviewed historical and recent research on MSI and other overlapping labels. Some of the key lessons learned from this review include immediate research priorities in the field, and here I provide a summary of the main gaps and areas for future research. It is important to stress that these areas concern both *what* we choose to research and also *how* we do research on MSI. Concerning what the focus of future research should be, I identified plenty of gaps, as expected for a field that is generally underresearched, but here I have chosen to focus only on those that are in my view the most urgent. The first issue is lack of a robust evidence base on successful interventions. Simply put, there are many approaches currently being used in practice that are very popular, but there is very limited research on their effectiveness for the specific population of MSI. This is a major gap in our knowledge, because many of these approaches have been developed for people with complex communication needs, but no sensory impairment(s) and when implemented in the context of MSI some adaptations are necessary (e.g. tactile methods). Examples of approaches popular with practitioners, but with little or no evidence base include, but are not limited to, AAC systems, intensive interaction, multisensory story making and telling, the role of other senses (e.g. smell and taste), and music-based interventions. It is relevant to also highlight that, where evidence on effectiveness exists, it may arise from the study of other age groups and settings – for example, adult populations in the case of intensive interaction, as shown in Chapter 4. There is also a rapidly increasing body of research on MSI focused on adults, and I argued that further research should also seek to prioritize focusing on children and young people. Furthermore, we need more research on MSI and mainstream schools, as most of the research conducted so far has been done with children and young people placed in special settings. To sum up, it is important to know how an intervention works and if it is effective in the narrow context of MSI and education, and this should include exploration of its use in a range of settings and across different age-groups, levels of ability and need.

The second major gap in knowledge that I have identified concerns the lack of data and perspectives from contexts, on which very little is currently known regarding MSI and education. Although not exhaustive, the review of international literature only identified one study from Brazil focusing exclusively on MSI. Given the challenges in searching and identifying the relevant literature, associated mainly with lack of common terminology and definition, and overlapping labels that I discussed in Chapter 2, it is almost certain that studies on MSI from other contexts do exist, although they probably have been published in languages other than English, and this may be the reason why I was not able to identify them. Even if this is the case, it is nevertheless evident that the vast majority of research on MSI has been conducted in Northern contexts (mainly the UK, US, Canada, Netherlands and some Nordic countries). It follows that from a mainstream Northern perspective, we currently know very little about MSI in Southern contexts, and this is a major gap, because these contexts have very particular characteristics. In Southern contexts, disability continuously interacts with a plethora of other factors that cause and perpetuate exclusion from education and society, such as forced migration, poverty and social inequality. It is necessary and urgent to explore MSI in these contexts in order to expand our knowledge on the role that complex intersections between disability and contextual factors play in shaping how inclusion and exclusion are experienced at the local level. The understanding and operationalization of inclusive education in Southern contexts is the other strand of my research alongside my passion for MSI (see for example, Kamenopoulou 2018). While working on different projects on inclusive education in Southern contexts, such as Colombia, Latin America and Bhutan, South Asia, I discovered that children and young people with MSI in these contexts are taught by specialists in special settings and they do not attend mainstream schools even if they do not have any additional cognitive impairment. We know very little about how children and young people learn in those special settings, what works best, what does not work so well and needs to be improved, and what support is needed. We moreover need to know how many children with MSI are out of school, either because of stigma associated with local perceptions of disability or because of the cultural context that prioritizes participation of children with disabilities in the community rather than in education. For example, in the case of rural Bhutan, society values a person with disabilities according to how able they are to contribute to their family's daily agricultural or household chores and not according to how successful they are in education. Finally, we need to focus on best practices and examples of successful inclusion in these contexts that are informed by local histories, traditions and belief systems, such as for example indigenous approaches, and effective models that respond to local needs and realities, such as for example interventions designed for those who have been the victims of war and violence or those living in poverty. Some useful questions we should be asking include: How do local models respond to local needs and what can the North learn from the South? As I have argued previously (see Kamenopoulou 2020), inclusive education is a field dominated by knowledge about the North, and very little is known about how inclusion and exclusion are experienced in the South. Almost nothing is known about how children with MSI experience inclusion in education (or not) in these contexts, hence we urgently need to start filling this major knowledge gap.

Regarding *how* we do research on MSI, as I stressed in Chapter 2, we desperately and urgently need to include the voices of children and young people with MSI and their families, including parents and siblings. The vast majority of research that has been carried out so far does not include their perspectives, but relies on data collected predominantly through researcher observations and interviews with practitioners. While acknowledging the challenges in developing inclusive and participatory research approaches, in Chapter 4, I made a clear case for why we need to further develop our repertoire of methods that show evidence of effectiveness in engaging children and young people with MSI in research, the value of doing so, and I also presented some strategies that can help us do that, including using approaches that allow for flexibility and necessary adaptations. It is useful to remember that everyone can communicate, including those with complex communication needs, such as children and young people with MSI and additional needs. The onus is on the researcher to find appropriate ways of establishing communication and rapport and to ensure that they include the child or young person's perspective, and ultimately listen to their voice (and that of their parents). Future research should seek to develop new and innovative strategies and to systematize existing bespoke methods – for example, by combining accessible methods for gathering the views and experiences of children and young people with other sources of information, such as teachers, parents, observations and other measurements. I stressed the need for triangulation of sources and cross-checking of different data in Chapters 2 and 4. This is particularly relevant to research on MSI, which almost always focuses on small and heterogeneous samples that render the application of quantitative research designs meaningless. Single and multiple qualitative case studies have traditionally been used in the field, simply due to the nature and size of the population, and one of the golden rules of good qualitative case study research is ensuring triangulation, which in turn maximizes the rigour and credibility of the findings and conclusions drawn (see Yin 2014; Kamenopoulou 2016).

5.2 Theory: what do we need to think about better or more?

As I clearly explained in Chapter 1, but also throughout this book, internationally a commonly accepted definition of deafblindness does not exist and the terminology used varies from one national context to another, and even within the same country. As a result, there are many common misconceptions about who is deafblind (and who is not); nor has this been clearly defined legally in many contexts. Moreover, there is a lack of awareness not only in the general population, but also among professionals, who work in education, social care and health. Consequently, deafblindness remains an invisible and misunderstood disability and deafblind children and young people's needs remain unidentified while they are being left behind. Lack of understanding of the specific needs of this distinct group of children and young people leads to barriers to communication and participation, with clear implications for their future developmental outcomes. The first global report on the situation of people with deafblindness confirms that this is the unfortunate reality across countries of the North and South. Indeed, in the list of recommendations arising from the report, it is clearly stated that one of the pre-conditions for inclusion is 'a universal and national recognition of deafblindness as a distinct disability in law and practice' and the adoption of 'a consistent definition and measurement of deafblindness' (World Federation of the Deafblind 2018: 48). Only when this is achieved, will the international community succeed in its ongoing efforts to implement the UNCRPD and to meet the SDGs in relation to children and young people with MSI.

The second area, on which more theoretical work is needed, is an understanding of MSI from a bioecological systems theory perspective that sees development as the result of complex and continuous interactions between an individual and their environment. As I demonstrated in Chapter 3, this is in line with the ICF model of disability and the capability approach, both of which stress the role of biology, ecology and psychology in development. This way of perceiving disability has been explored very little in specific relation to MSI (see Kamenopoulou 2016), and in Chapter 3, I tried to do just that by presenting a conceptualization of social development in the context of MSI from a bioecological systems perspective. Developing an understanding of all areas of development from a bioecological systems perspective is an area on which future theory on MSI could focus. Future work could also seek to theorize about the usefulness of combining elements from a range of relevant theories, such as sociocultural, attachment and social learning and deprivation theories, which I critically discussed in Chapter 3, as well as other theories that have been proposed as useful in the context of MSI, and that were not covered in this book. For example, as I mentioned in Chapter 2, van Dijk's work with deafblind children has also been influenced by Piaget's theory of cognitive development, and strategies informed by behaviourism, such as using prompting, repetitions and reinforcement, are relevant to MSI. However, it is interesting to point out that in relation to teaching self-care skills, Meshcheryakov (1979) rejected the behaviourist approach, arguing that the aim should not be to train the child by mere mechanical repetition, but to encourage them to satisfy their needs, and this is a contradiction that deserves to be further explored.

Finally, Maslow's hierarchy of needs (Sirgy 1986) is a theory that has been applied to the context of MSI (Lachney 2018) to show that deafblind individuals are prevented from having a quality of life, because they are not enabled to satisfy their needs, from the most basic physiological needs (e.g. food, warmth) through to the most elaborate self-fulfilment needs (e.g. achieving one's full potential, including self-expression and creative activities). The main idea behind this framework is that a person is able to progress to stages of higher level needs, only once they have met the earlier and more basic stages. It is indeed the case that many deafblind individuals, who have appropriate support, live fulfilling lives and achieve their full potential. Molly Watt, who has Ushers syndrome, and with her work raises awareness about the condition and the importance of assistive technology and accessibility for deafblind people, and Haben Girma, the first deafblind woman, who graduated from Harvard Law and a disability rights lawyer and advocate, are just two illustrative examples worthy of mention. Maslow's hierarchy of needs can indeed be a helpful framework for conceptualizing the extent to which children and young people with MSI are included and take part in education, and if barriers to inclusion and participation prevent them from satisfying their needs, such as for example, establishing friendships to satisfy their social needs. All theories mentioned in this book should be further explored in the context of MSI, because having a solid theoretical framework for the ways in which the human mind, body and psyche develops, when vision and hearing are absent or impaired, will be a really valuable basis for future research and practice.

5.3 Practice: what do we need to do better or more?

The first recommendation in relation to future practice may also be seen as a key priority for future research or, to put it more accurately, as an opportunity for exciting new collaborations between practice and research. The rapid expansion of technology and the internet over the last few years has led to innovative approaches that ensure access, support communication and meet the needs of people with disabilities, including those who are deafblind. For example, mobile devices, such as phones and tablets now have applications that eliminate barriers, by converting speech to text or by identifying accessible venues. Moreover, social media applications can enable communication and greater social participation of deafblind people (in one of her speeches, Haben Girma described how she messaged a classmate through Facebook to introduce herself, because the classmate did not know how to initiate a conversation with her when they met). In addition, there are applications that education professionals can use – for example, during assessment, that can help minimize the time spent recording and processing data, and make storage and sharing of relevant information straightforward. These approaches deserve to be explored more in practice, but also in research. As Hodges et al. (2019) point out, some of the existing research on assistive technology and MSI concerns devices and methods that are now considered outdated. Exploring the possibilities offered by innovative technology more systematically will open the doors to greater interaction of deafblind people with the world.

The most important recommendation for the improvement of future practice is the universal need for teacher *training* specifically on MSI, which is again in line with the first global report on deafblindness. In Chapter 3 and throughout this book, I described the very distinctive needs of children and young people with MSI, as well as the great heterogeneity of the population, depending on the complex interactions between various factors, both of which render deafblindness a unique and complex disability. Moreover, in Chapter 4, I presented a range of specialized communication methods available for people with deafblindness, and a variety of strategies and approaches that education professionals can use to support and encourage communication, mobility and orientation, and acquisition of information about the environment. I argued that all these strategies should be part of every teacher's repertoire, and here I will explain why.

As discussed in Chapter 1, the 1994 Salamanca Statement stipulated that the preparation of teaching personnel is a key factor contributing to the success of inclusive education. It proposed that all standard teacher training courses should cover disability awareness and the skills required to respond to special educational needs, and that a standard teaching qualification should be a requirement for those completing any further specialized training courses. Finally, it stressed the central role that universities have in creating training programmes and materials. On the other hand, Article 24 of the UNCRPD, which specifically mentions deafblindness, calls on states to ensure that the education of children with single or dual sensory impairment is delivered in the most appropriate *means of communication* and in educational environments that support their academic achievement and social development. Regardless of the mainstream versus special placement debate, it follows that to be able to include children and young people with MSI in any education setting, teachers and other professionals need training on inclusive approaches, such as guidance on how to implement UDL to make their lessons accessible to all, but also further specialized training on MSI, including the use of appropriate communication methods, and the arrangement of necessary adaptations to the educational environment. If this is achieved, then education professionals will have the confidence, knowledge and skills required to better support the inclusion and participation of children with MSI in any educational setting, mainstream or special, depending on what option best suits each child's unique profile.

Finally, on the wider societal sphere, raising awareness about MSI will support greater inclusion. Increasing the visibility of deafblind people is key, and for this to happen, it is essential that they are invited to contribute to any training or awareness-raising initiatives, so that their voices and experiences can inform a better and more complete understanding of their needs – for example, regarding the elimination of access barriers in different contexts. The lack of training on MSI is the main reason behind a new asynchronous course (i.e. pre-recorded materials that trainees can work through in their own time) for professionals that I developed in collaboration with the Centre for Inclusive Education (CIE), at IOE, UCL, which is a research centre focusing on the link between research and practice and on actively promoting knowledge exchange on special educational needs, inclusion, and disability between academia and different audiences. The short course is designed to teach the basics that everyone should know about MSI, such as for example, what it is and what it is not, dispelling some of the myths that surround this little known and less understood disability, its main causes, and importantly, guidance on how to assess and structure the environment to ensure access, as well as the main strategies for communicating and interacting with a deafblind person. The piloting of the short course is currently ongoing with a group of professionals, and based on their feedback, it will be finalized and made available to the public within 2022. The course has already received a lot of interest from professionals (not just in education but also from health and social care services or in public facing institutions, such as museums), and I have already adapted it to create a synchronous training course (delivered live), to suit different trainee needs and circumstances. My ongoing work with CIE also includes the development and delivery of bespoke and more specialized and detailed courses, depending on the trainees' particular requirements and circumstances.

As I explained in Chapter 1, the current lack of resources on MSI for teachers, other professionals, students and researchers was the rationale behind this book and my main motivator during the long and complicated process of writing it. As 'persons with deafblindness are still left behind in all countries of the world' (World Federation of the Deafblind 2018: 49), I argue that universities have responsibility to conduct more work on developing specialized training, awareness-raising courses and useful resources on MSI, and that governments have responsibility to provide more funding for this important and necessary work, because this will lead to more effective overall support for all children and young people, better developmental outcomes, and ultimately, their greater inclusion and participation in education and the wider society.

Appendix: Useful websites

UK-wide

Amber Trust

https://ambertrust.org
Amber Sound Touch project: https://soundtouch.ambertrust.org

British Deaf Association

https://bda.org.uk

Communication Matters

www.communicationmatters.org.uk

Deafblind Scotland

https://dbscotland.org.uk

Deafblind UK

https://deafblind.org.uk

Intensive Interaction Institute

www.intensiveinteraction.org

Molly Watt Trust

www.mollywatt.com/molly-watt-trust

National Deaf Children's Society

www.ndcs.org.uk

Royal National Institute for the Blind

www.rnib.org.uk
Talking Books: www.rnib.org.uk/talking-books-service

Royal National Institute for Deaf people
https://rnid.org.uk

Royal Society for Blind Children
www.rsbc.org.uk

Scope UK
www.scope.org.uk

Scottish Sensory Centre
www.ssc.education.ed.ac.uk

Sense Scotland
www.sensescotland.org.uk

Sense UK
www.sense.org.uk

Vision Impairment Centre for Teaching and Research (VICTAR)
www.birmingham.ac.uk/research/victar/about/index.aspx

International

Academic Collaborative Centre for PIMD (ACC-PIMD), The Netherlands
https://aw-emb.nl/en

CHARGE Lab, Central Michigan University, USA
https://stage-www.cmich.edu/academics/colleges/liberal-arts-social-sciences/departments/psychology/psychology-centers-clinics-research-labs/charge-lab

Daisy Consortium
https://daisy.org

Deafblind International
www.deafblindinternational.org

Appendix

European Deafblind Network
https://edbn.org

European Deafblind Union
www.edbu.eu

Institute for Deafblindness (UGIDB), University of Groningen, The Netherlands
www.rug.nl/gmw/pedagogical-and-educational-sciences/research/ugidb/

International Society for Alternative and Augmentative Communication
https://isaac-online.org/english/home/

National Centre on Deaf-Blindness, USA
www.nationaldb.org

National Library Service for the Blind and Print Disabled, Washington, USA
www.loc.gov/nls/

Perkins School for the Blind, Boston, USA
www.perkins.org

Research in dual sensory loss/deafblindness, Orebro University, Sweden
www.oru.se/english/research/research-teams/rt/?rdb=g252

Sense International
www.senseinternational.org.uk

Sightsavers
www.sightsavers.org

Touch Base: Center for the Deafblind, Houston, Texas
www.touchbasecenter.org

Usher Syndrome Society

www.ushersyndromesociety.org

World Federation of the Deafblind

www.wfdb.eu

References

Aitken, S. (2000a). Deafblindness and society, in S. Aitken, M. Buultjens, C. Clark, J.T. Eyre and L. Pease (eds) *Teaching Children who are Deafblind: Contact, Communication and Learning*. David Fulton Publishers, pp. 200–34.

Aitken, S. (2000b). Understanding deafblindness, in S. Aitken, M. Buultjens, C. Clark, J.T. Eyre and L. Pease (eds) *Teaching Children who are Deafblind: Contact, Communication and Learning*. David Fulton Publishers, pp. 1–34.

Aitken, S., Buultjens, M., Clark, C., Eyre, J.T. and Pease, L. (eds) (2000). *Teaching Children who are Deafblind: Contact, Communication and Learning*. David Fulton Publishers.

Aitken, S. and Millar, S. (2004). *Listening to Children*. Sense Scotland.

Ali, E., MacFarland, S.Z. and Umbrette, J. (2011). Effectiveness of combining tangible symbols with the Picture Exchange Communication System to teach requesting skills to children with multiple disabilities including visual impairment. *Education and Training in Autism and Developmental Disabilities*, 46(3): 425–35. Available at: www.jstor.org/stable/23880596 [accessed 10 June 2022].

Argyropoulou, Z. and Papoudi, D. (2012). The training of a child with autism in a Greek preschool inclusive class through intensive interaction: A case study, *European Journal of Special Needs Education*, 27(1): 99–114. doi: 10.1080/08856257.2011.640489

Arnold, P. and Leadley, J. (1999). Tactile memory of deafblind participants, *Deafness & Education International*, 1(2): 108–13. doi: 10.1179/146431599790561415

Arter, C., Mason, H., McCall, S., McLinden, M. and Stone, J. (1999). *Children with Visual Impairment in Mainstream Settings*. David Fulton Publishers.

Avramidis, E. and Norwich, B. (2002). Teachers' attitudes towards integration/inclusion: A review of the literature, *European Journal of Special Needs Education*, 17(2): 129–47. doi: 10.1080/08856250210129056

Bakhurst, D. (1991). *Consciousness and Revolution in Soviet Philosophy: From the Bolsheviks to Evald Ilyenkov*. Cambridge University Press.

Bakhurst, D. and Padden, C. (1991). The Meshcheryakov experiment: Soviet work on the education of blind-deaf children, *Learning and Instruction*, 1(3): 201–15.

Bandura, A. (1977). *Social Learning Theory*. Prentice Hall.

Barber, M. (2008). Using intensive interaction to add to the palette of interactive possibilities in teacher–pupil communication, *European Journal of Special Needs Education*, 23(4): 393–402. doi: 10.1080/08856250802387380

Boas, D.C.V., Ferreira, L.P., De Moura, M.C., Maia, S.R. and Amaral, I. (2016). Analysis of interaction and attention processes in a child with congenital deafblindness, *American Annals of the Deaf*, 161(3): 327–41. doi: 10.1353/aad.2016.0025

Boothroyd, E. (1997). *Extra Sensory Support: A Survey of Education Services for Deafblind and Multi-sensory-impaired Children in Local Education Authorities and Specialist Schools in England and Wales*. Sense.

Bowlby, J. (1991). *Attachment and Loss*. Penguin Books.

Boyle, C., Topping, C. and Jindal-Snape, D. (2013). Teachers' attitudes towards inclusion in high schools, *Teachers and Teaching: Theory and Practice*, 19(5): 527–42. doi: 10.1080/13540602.2013.827361

Bozic, N. and Murdoch, H. (eds) (1996). *Learning Through Interaction: Technology and Children with Multiple Disabilities*. David Fulton Publishers.

Brigg, G., Schuitema, K. and Vorhaus, J. (2016). Children with profound and multiple learning difficulties: Laughter, capability and relating to others, *Disability & Society*, 31(9): 1175–89. doi: 10.1080/09687599.2016.1239571

Bronfenbrenner, U. (1979). *The Ecology of Human Development: Experiments by Nature and Design*. Harvard University Press.

Bronfenbrenner, U. (2005). The bioecological theory of human development, in U. Bronfenbrenner (ed.) *Making Human Beings Human: Bioecological Perspectives on Human Development*. Sage Publications, pp. 3–15.

Bronfenbrenner, U. and Morris, P.A. (2006). The bioecological model of human development, in R.M. Lerner and W. Damon (eds) *Handbook of Child Psychology: Theoretical Models of Human Development*, 6th edn. John Wiley & Sons, pp. 793–828.

Bruce, S.M. and Borders, C. (2015). Communication and language in learners who are deaf and hard of hearing with disabilities: Theories, research, and practice, *American Annals of the Deaf*, 160(4): 368–84. Available at: www.jstor.org/stable/10.2307/26235228 [accessed 10 June 2022].

Bruce, S.M., Nelson, C., Perez, A., Stutzman, B. and Barnhill, B.A. (2016). The state of research on communication and literacy in deafblindness, *American Annals of the Deaf*, 161(4): 424–43.

Bruner, J. (1990). *Acts of Meaning*. Harvard University Press.

Buckley, W. (2003). Computer activities to support communication and language development in children who are Deafblind, *Deaf-Blind Perspectives*, 11(1): 7–12. Available at: https://documents.nationaldb.org/dbp/pdf/sept03.pdf#page=7 [accessed 5 April 2022].

Bunning, K., Smith, C., Kennedy, P. and Greenham, C. (2013). Examination of the communication interface between students with severe to profound and multiple intellectual disability and educational staff during structured teaching sessions, *Journal of Intellectual Disability Research*, 57(1): 39–52. doi: 10.1111/j.1365-2788.2011.01513.x

Burman, E. (2004). Language talk, in H. Daniels and A. Edwards (eds) *The Routledge Falmer Reader in Psychology of Education*. Routledge, pp. 51–66.

Buultjens, M., Stead, J. and Dallas, M. (2001). *Promoting Social Inclusion of Pupils with Visual Impairment in Mainstream Schools in Scotland*. Scottish Sensory Centre.

Byrne, B. (2019). How inclusive is the right to inclusive education? An assessment of the UN convention on the rights of persons with disabilities: Concluding observations, *International Journal of Inclusive Education*, 26(3): 301–18. doi: 10.1080/13603116.2019.1651411

Capp, M.J. (2017). The effectiveness of Universal Design for Learning: A meta-analysis of literature between 2013 and 2016, *International Journal of Inclusive Education*, 21(8): 791–807. doi: 10.1080/13603116.2017.1325074

Chadwick, D., Buell, S. and Goldbart, J. (2019). Approaches to communication assessment with children and adults with profound intellectual and multiple disabilities, *Journal of Applied Research in Intellectual Disabilities*, 32(2): 336–58.

Chen, D., Downing, J. and Rodriguez-Gil, G. (2000). Tactile learning strategies for children who are deaf-blind: Concerns and considerations from project SALUTE, *Deaf-Blind Perspectives*, 8(2): 1–6.

Chu, S.-Y. and Lo, Y.-L.S. (2016). Taiwanese families' perspectives on learning disabilities: An exploratory study in three middle schools, *Journal of Research in Special Educational Needs*, 16(2): 77–88. doi: 10.1111/1471-3802.12058

Cigman, R. (2007). A question of universality: Inclusive education and the principle of respect, *Journal of Philosophy of Education*, 41(4): 775–93. doi: 10.1111/j.1467-9752.2007.00577.x

Clark, C. (2000). Personal and social development, in S. Aitken, M. Buultjens, C. Clark, J.T. Eyre and L. Pease (eds) *Teaching Children who are Deafblind: Contact, Communication and Learning*. David Fulton Publishers, pp. 83–118.

References

Croll, P. and Moses, D. (2000). Ideologies and utopias: Education professionals' views of inclusion, *European Journal of Special Needs Education*, 15(1): 1–12. doi: 10.1080/088562500361664

Dammeyer, J. (2014). Deafblindness: A review of the literature, *Scandinavian Journal of Public Health*, 42(7): 554–62. doi: 10.1177/1403494814544399

Dammeyer, J. and Ask Larsen, F. (2016). Communication and language profiles of children with congenital deafblindness, *British Journal of Visual Impairment*, 34(3): 214–24. doi: 10.1177/0264619616651301

Daniels, H. (2001). *Vygotsky and Pedagogy*. Routledge.

de Boer, A.A. and Munde, V.S. (2015). Parental attitudes toward the inclusion of children with profound intellectual and multiple disabilities in general primary education in the Netherlands, *Journal of Special Education*, 49(3): 179–87. doi: 10.1177/0022466914554297

DeCaluwe, S., McLetchie, B., Luiselli, T.E., Mason, B. and Peters, H. (1999). Communication Portfolio: A tool to increase the competence of communication partners of learners who are deaf-blind, *Deaf-Blind Perspectives*, 11(3): 5–8.

Department for Education and Department of Health and Social Care (DfE and DHSC) (2015). *SEND Code of Practice 0–25 Years: Statutory Guidance for Organisations which Work with and Support Children and Young People who have Special Educational Needs or Disabilities*. Available at: https://assets.publishing.service.gov.uk/government/uploads/system/uploads/attachment_data/file/398815/SEND_Code_of_Practice_January_2015.pdf [accessed 10 June 2022].

Department of Health (DoH) (1997). *Think Dual Sensory: Good Practice Guidelines for Older People with Dual Sensory Loss*. The Stationery Office.

Department of Health (DoH) (2014). *Care and Support for Deafblind Children and Adults Policy Guidance*. Available at: https://assets.publishing.service.gov.uk/government/uploads/system/uploads/attachment_data/file/388198/Care_and_Support_for_Deafblind_Children_and_Adults_Policy_Guidance_12_12_14_FINAL.pdf [accessed 10 June 2022].

Deuce, G. (2017). The education of learners with CHARGE syndrome, *British Journal of Special Education*, 44(4): 376–93. doi: 10.1111/1467-8578.12183

Deuce, G., Howard, S., Rose, S. and Fuggle, C. (2012). A study of CHARGE syndrome in the UK, *British Journal of Visual Impairment*, 30(2): 91–100. doi: 10.1177/0264619612443883

Douglas, G. and McLinden, M. (2005). Visual impairment, in A. Lewis and B. Norwich (eds) *Special Teaching for Special Children?: Pedagogies for Inclusion*. Open University Press, pp. 26–40.

Downing, J. and Eichinger, J. (1990). Instructional strategies for learners with dual sensory impairments in integrated settings, *Journal of the Association of Persons with Severe Handicaps*, 15(2): 98–105.

Dunnett, J. (1990). A visual assessment of a young multiply handicapped girl and an associated teaching programme, *Child: Care, Health and Development*, 16(6): 355–63.

Ellinor, J. (2019). It's the 'group' that matters: Dramatherapy working with a group of parents and their children who have profound and multiple learning difficulties, *Dramatherapy*, 40(1): 5–16. doi: 10.1177/0263067219834697

Evans, J. and Lunt, I. (2002). Inclusive education: Are there limits?, *European Journal of Special Needs Education*, 17(1): 1–14. doi: 10.1080/08856250110098980

Eyre, J.T. (2000). Holistic assessment, in S. Aitken, M. Buultjens, C. Clark, J.T. Eyre and L. Pease (eds) *Teaching Children who are Deafblind: Contact, Communication and Learning*. David Fulton Publishers, pp. 119–40.

References

Foster, S.B. and DeCaro, P.M. (1991). An ecological model of social interaction between deaf and hearing students within a postsecondary educational setting, *Disability, Handicap and Society*, 6(3): 181–201. doi: 10.1080/02674649166780241

Fraiberg, S. (1977). *Insights from the Blind*. Souvenir Press.

Freeman, P. (1975). *Understanding the Deaf-blind Child*. Heinemann Health Books.

French, S. (1993). Disability, impairment or something in between?, in J. Swain, V. Finkelstein, S. French and M. Oliver (eds) *Disabling Barriers—Enabling Environment*. Sage Publications; Open University Press, pp. 17–25.

Ganz, J.B., Simpson, R.L. and Corbin-Newsome, J. (2008). The impact of the Picture Exchange Communication System on requesting and speech development in pre-schoolers with autism spectrum disorders and similar characteristics, *Research in Autism Spectrum Disorders*, 2(1): 157–69. doi: 10.1016/j.rasd.2007.04.005

Giangreco, M.F., Cloninger, C.J., Mueller, P.H., Yuan, S. and Ashworth, S. (1991). Perspectives of parents whose children have dual sensory impairments, *Journal of the Association for Persons with Severe Handicaps*, 16(1): 14–24.

Girma, H. (2019). *Haben: The Deafblind Woman who Conquered Harvard Law*. Hachette UK.

Glidden Prickett, J. and Rafalowski Welch, T. (1998). Educating students who are deafblind, in S.Z. Sacks and R.K. Silberman (eds) *Educating Students who have Visual Impairments with Other Disabilities*. Paul H. Brookes Publishing, pp. 139–60.

Goldbart, J. and Caton, S. (2010). *Communication and People with the Most Complex Needs: What Works and Why this is Essential* (Full Report). Manchester Research Metropolitan University (MMU), Institute for Health and Social Change.

Goldbart, J., Chadwick, D. and Buell, S. (2014). Speech and language therapists' approaches to communication intervention with children and adults with profound and multiple learning disability, *International Journal of Language & Communication Disorders*, 49(6): 687–701.

Haakma, I., Janssen, M. and Minnaert, A. (2016). Understanding the relationship between teacher behavior and motivation in students with acquired deafblindness, *American Annals of the Deaf*, 161(3): 314–26.

Harding, C., Lindsay, G., O'Brien, A., Dipper, L. and Wright, J. (2011). Implementing AAC with children with profound and multiple learning disabilities: A study in rationale underpinning intervention, *Journal of Research in Special Educational Needs*, 11(2): 120–9. doi: 10.1111/j.1471-3802.2010.01184.x

Haring, T.G., Haring, N., Breen, C., Romer, L.T. and White, J. (1995). Social relationships among students with deaf-blindness and their peers in inclusive settings, in N.G. Haring and L.T. Romer (eds) *Welcoming Students who are Deaf-Blind into Typical Classrooms: Facilitating School Participation, Learning, and Friendships*. Paul H. Brookes, pp. 231–48.

Harris, J.R. (1998). *The Nurture Assumption: Why Children Turn Out the Way they Do*. Free Press.

Hartmann, E. and Weismer, P. (2016). Technology implementation and curriculum engagement for children and youth who are deafblind, *American Annals of the Deaf*, 161(4): 462–73. Available at: www.jstor.org/stable/10.2307/26235296 [accessed 10 June 2022].

Hartshorne, T.S. and Schmittel, M.C. (2016). Social-emotional development in children and youth who are deafblind, *American Annals of the Deaf*, 161(4): 444–53. Available at: www.jstor.org/stable/10.2307/26235294 [accessed 10 June 2022].

Hayton, J. and Dimitriou, D. (2019). What's in a word? Distinguishing between Habilitation and Re-habilitation, *International Journal of Orientation and Mobility*, 10(1): 1–4. https://doi.org/10.21307/ijom-2019-007

Hayton, J. and Mort, S. (2022). Orientation, mobility, and independence skills: Habilitation approaches, in N. Dale, A. Salt, J. Sargent and R. Greenaway (eds) *Children with Vision Impairment: Assessment, Development and Management*. Mac Keith Press, pp. 173–85.

Heller, K.W., Alberto, P.A. and Bowdin, J. (1995). Interactions of communication partners and students who are deaf-blind: A model, *Journal of Visual Impairment & Blindness*, 89(5): 391–401.

Hendrickson, H. and McLinden, M. (1995). Study of raised symbolic communication systems for visually impaired people with additional learning difficulties, *International Journal of Language & Communication Disorders*, 30(S1): 526–33.

Hewett, D. (ed.) (2018). *The Intensive Interaction Handbook*, 2nd edn. Sage Publications.

Hirstwood, R. and Smith, C. (1996). Developing competencies in multi-sensory rooms, in N. Bozic and H. Murdoch (eds) *Learning Through Interaction: Technology and Children with Multiple Disabilities*. David Fulton Publishers, pp. 83–91.

Hitchins, A.R. and Hogan, S.C. (2018). Outcomes of early intervention for deaf children with additional needs following an auditory verbal approach to communication, *International Journal of Pediatric Otorhinolaryngology*, 115: 125–32. doi: 10.1016/j.ijporl.2018.09.025

Hodges, E.M. (2004). Learning styles in deafblind children: Perspectives from practice. Doctoral thesis, University of Birmingham. UBIRA ETheses repository. Available at: https://etheses.bham.ac.uk/id/eprint/12/1/Hodges04PhD.pdf [accessed 10 June 2022].

Hodges, E. and McLinden, M. (2014). Learners with severe and profound learning difficulties and sensory impairments, in P. Lacey, R. Ashdown, P. Jones, H. Lawson and M. Pipe (eds) *The Routledge Companion to Severe, Profound and Multiple Learning Difficulties*. Taylor & Francis Group, pp. 153–62. doi: 10.4324/9781315717913

Hodges, L. (2000). Effective teaching and learning, in S. Aitken, M. Buultjens, C. Clark, J.T. Eyre and L. Pease (eds) *Teaching Children who are Deafblind: Contact, Communication and Learning*. David Fulton Publishers, pp. 167–99.

Hodges, L., Ellis, L., Douglas, G. et al. (2019). *A Rapid Evidence Assessment of the Effectiveness of Educational Interventions to Support Children and Young People with Multi-sensory Impairment*. Welsh Government. GSR report number 51/2019. Available at: https://gov.wales/sites/default/files/statistics-and-research/2019-11/effectiveness-educational-interventions-support-children-young-people-multi-sensory-impairment.pdf [accessed 10 June 2022].

Hodkinson, A. (2019). *Key Issues in Special Educational Needs, Disability & Inclusion*, 3rd edn. SAGE.

Hornby, G. (2015). Inclusive special education: Development of a new theory for the education of children with special educational needs and disabilities, *British Journal of Special Education*, 42(3): 234–56. doi: 10.1111/1467-8578.12101

Huebner, K.M., Kirchner, C. and Prickett, J.G. (1995). Meeting personnel training needs: The deaf-blind self-study curriculum project, *Journal of Visual Impairment & Blindness*, 89(3): 235–43.

Hutchinson, N. and Bodycoat, A. (2015). The effectiveness of intensive interaction, a systematic literature review, *Journal of Applied Research in Intellectual Disabilities*, 28(6): 437–54. doi: 10.1111/jar.12138

Imray, P. and Colley, A. (2017). *Inclusion is Dead: Long Live Inclusion*. Routledge Focus.

Jaiswal, A., Aldersey, H., Wittich, W., Mirza, M. and Finlayson, M. (2018). Participation experiences of people with deafblindness or dual sensory loss: A scoping review of global deafblind literature, *PloS One*, 13(9): e0203772. https://doi.org/10.1371/journal.pone.0203772

Jaiswal, A., Aldersey, H.M., Wittich, W., Mirza, M. and Finlayson, M. (2020). Meaning and experiences of participation: A phenomenological study with persons with deafblindness in India, *Disability and Rehabilitation*, 42(18): 2580–92. doi: 10.1080/09638288.2018.1564943

Jamieson, J.R. (1995). Interactions between mothers and children who are deaf, *Journal of Early Intervention*, 19(2): 108–17.

Janssen, M.J., Riksen-Walraven, J.M. and Van Dijk, J.P.M. (2003). Toward a diagnostic intervention model for fostering harmonious interactions between deaf-blind children and their educators, *Journal of Visual Impairment & Blindness*, 97(4): 197–214.

Jarvis, J., Sinka, I. and Iantaffi, A. (2002). Inclusion – what deaf pupils think: An RNID/DfES project undertaken by the University of Hertfordshire, November 2001 – July 2002, *Deafness & Education International*, 4(3): 142–7. doi: 10.1179/146431502790560836

Kamenopoulou, L. (2004). Teaching children who are deafblind in mainstream educational settings. Master's thesis, Graduate School of Education, University of Bristol.

Kamenopoulou, L. (2005). Challenging behaviour and deafblindness: A critical review of the literature, *SLD Experience*, 42: 15–22.

Kamenopoulou, L. (2009). Social inclusion of deafblind young people: Exploring peer interactions and relationships in mainstream secondary schools. Doctoral thesis, Institute of Education, University College London.

Kamenopoulou, L. (2012). A study on the inclusion of deafblind young people in mainstream schools: Key findings and implications for research and practice, *British Journal of Special Education*, 39(3): 137–45. doi: 10.1111/j.1467-8578.2012.00546.x

Kamenopoulou, L. (2016). Ecological systems theory: A valuable framework for research on inclusion and special educational needs/disabilities, *Pedagogy and GLOBI*, 88(4): 515–27.

Kamenopoulou, L. (ed.) (2018). *Inclusive Education and Disability in the Global South: Research from Belize, Bhutan, Malaysia and Philippines*. Palgrave Macmillan. https://doi.org/10.1007/978-3-319-72829-2

Kamenopoulou, L. (2020). Decolonising inclusive education: An example from a research in Colombia, *Disability and the Global South*, 7(1): 1792–812. Available at: https://disabilityglobalsouth.files.wordpress.com/2020/05/07_01_01.pdf [accessed 4 April 2022].

Kamenopoulou, L., Ali, A. and Ockelford, A. (2021). Multi-sensory impairment: Convenient label or recipe for confusion? A scoping review of research conducted in England (2001–20), *Journal of Research in Special Educational Needs*, 21(2): 98–110. doi: 10.1111/1471-3802.12503

Kamenopoulou, L., Buli-Holmberg, J. and Siska, J. (2016). An exploration of student teachers' perspectives at the start of a post-graduate study programme on inclusion and special needs education, *International Journal of Inclusive Education*, 20(7): 743–55. doi: 10.1080/13603116.2015.1111445

Kartika, D. and Kuroda, K. (2019). Implications for teacher training and support for inclusive education: Empirical evidence from Cambodia, in M.J. Schuelka, C.J. Johnstone, G. Thomas and A.J. Artiles (eds) *The SAGE Handbook of Inclusion and Diversity in Education*. SAGE, pp. 446–67.

Keil, S. (2002). Survey of educational provision for blind and partially sighted children in England, Scotland and Wales in 2002, *British Journal of Visual Impairment*, 23(3): 93–7.

Keil, S. (2017). *Official Data on Children and Young People with Vision Impairment in England 2016. Briefing Report 1: Population Characteristics*. Royal National Institute for the Blind (RNIB). Available at: www.rnib.org.uk/sites/default/files/RNIB%20briefing%20on%20DfE%20SEN%20statistics%202016%20%28Population%29.docx [accessed 10 June 2022].

Kellett, M. (2003). Jacob's journey: Developing sociability and communication in a young boy with severe and complex learning difficulties using the intensive interaction teaching approach, *Journal of Research in Special Educational Needs*, 3(1): 1–16. https://doi-org.libproxy.ucl.ac.uk/10.1111/j.1471-3802.2003.00181.x

Kiuppis, F. (2014). Why (not) associate the principle of inclusion with disability? Tracing connections from the start of the 'Salamanca Process', *International Journal of Inclusive Education*, 18(7): 746–61. doi: 10.1080/13603116.2013.826289

Kunwar Deer, L. and Kamenopoulou, L. (2022). Disadvantage in the English SEN and disabilities system: Parents' perspectives through a 'theory of disadvantage' lens [article submitted for publication in *Disability & Society*].

Lacey, P. (2001). The role of learning support assistants in the inclusive learning of pupils with severe and profound learning difficulties, *Educational Review*, 53(2): 157–67. doi: 10.1080/00131910120055589

Lachney, S.K. (2018). Quality of life for deafblind individuals: Comparing the effect of living with and without support service providers. Master's thesis, Western Oregon University. Available at: https://digitalcommons.wou.edu/theses/47 [accessed 10 June 2022].

Laffan, C. (1997). Multiple disability and sight loss: Children, parents and professionals, *British Journal of Visual Impairment*, 15(3): 109–12.

Lagatti, S. (1995). 'Deaf-Blind' or 'deafblind'? International perspective on terminology, *Journal of Visual Impairment & Blindness*, 89(3): 306.

Lautenbach, F. and Heyder, A. (2019). Changing attitudes to inclusion in preservice teacher education: A systematic review, *Educational Research*, 61(2): 231–53. doi: 10.1080/00131881.2019.1596035

Lawson, H., Byers, R., Rayner, M., Aird, R. and Pease, L. (2015). Curriculum models, issues and tensions, in P. Lacey, R. Ashdown, P. Jones, H. Lawson and M. Pipe (eds) *The Routledge Companion to Severe, Profound and Multiple Learning Difficulties*. Routledge, pp. 233–45. Available at: www.routledgehandbooks.com/doi/10.4324/9781315717913.ch23 [accessed 10 June 2022].

Leontiev, A.H. (1948). *How I Form a Picture Around Me*. Progress Press.

Lewis, A. (2002). Accessing, through research interviews, the views of children with difficulties in learning, *Support for Learning*, 17(3): 111–16. https://doi.org/10.1111/1467-9604.00248

Lewis, A. (2004). 'And when did you last see your father?' Exploring the views of children with learning difficulties/disabilities, *British Journal of Special Education*, 31(1): 3–9. https://doi.org/10.1111/j.0952-3383.2004.00319.x

Lewis, A. (2009). Methodological issues in exploring the ideas of children with autism concerning self and spirituality, *Religion, Disability and Health*, 13(1): 64–76. https://doi.org/10.1080/15228960802581446

Lewis, A. (2010). Silence in the context of child 'voice', *Children and Society*, 24(1): 14–23. https://doi.org/10.1111/j.1099-0860.2008.00200.x

Lewis, A. (2011). FIVE disabled children's 'voice' and experiences, in S. Haines and D. Ruebain (eds) *Education, Disability and Social Policy*. Bristol Policy Press, pp. 89–104.

Lewis, V. (2003). *Development and Disability*. Blackwell.

Lieberman, L.J. (2002). Fitness for individuals who are visually impaired or Deafblind, *RE:view*, 34(1): 13–23. Available at: https://sites.aph.org/physical-education/articles/fitness-for-individuals-who-are-visually-impaired-or-deafblind/ [accessed 4 April 2022].

Lieberman, L.J. and Taule, J. (1997). Ways to incorporate physical fitness into the lives of individuals who are deaf-blind, *Deaf-Blind Perspectives*, 5(2): 6–10.

Little, S. and Dutton, G.N. (2015). Some children with multiple disabilities and cerebral visual impairment can engage when enclosed by a 'tent': Is this due to Balint syndrome?, *British Journal of Visual Impairment*, 33(1): 66–73. doi: 10.1177/0264619614553860

Llewellyn, A. and Hogan, K. (2000). The use and abuse of models of disability, *Disability & Society*, 15(1): 157–65. doi: 10.1080/09687590025829

Mar, H.H. and Sall, N. (1995). Enhancing social opportunities and relationships of children who are deaf-blind, *Journal of Visual Impairment & Blindness*, 89(3): 280–6.

Marschark, M. (1993). *Psychological Development of Deaf Children*. Oxford University Press.

McCall, S. and McLinden, M. (2001). Literacy and children who are blind and who have additional disabilities – the challenges for teachers and researchers, *International Journal of Disability, Development and Education*, 48(4): 355–75. doi: 10.1080/10349120120094266

McCall, S. and McLinden, M. (2007). Teachers' perspectives on the use of the Moon code to develop literacy in children with visual impairments and additional disabilities, *Journal of Visual Impairment & Blindness*, 101(10): 601–12.

McInnes, J.M. and Treffry, J.A. (1982). *Deaf-Blind Infants and Children: A Developmental Guide*. University of Toronto Press.

McLetchie, B. (1995). Teacher preparation, in N.G. Haring and L.T. Romer (eds) *Welcoming Students who are Deaf-blind into Typical Classrooms: Facilitating School Participation, Learning, and Friendships*. Paul H. Brookes, pp. 89–104.

McLinden, M. (1995). Touching the Moon, *British Journal of Special Education*, 22(2): 64–9.

McLinden, M. (1999). Hands on: Haptic exploratory strategies in children who are blind with multiple disabilities, *British Journal of Visual Impairment*, 17(1): 23–9.

McLinden, M. (2004). Haptic exploratory strategies and children who are blind and have additional disabilities, *Journal of Visual Impairment & Blindness*, 98(2): 99–115.

McLinden, M. (2012). Mediating haptic exploratory strategies in children who have visual impairment and intellectual disabilities, *Journal of Intellectual Disability Research*, 56(2): 129–39. doi: 10.1111/j.1365-2788.2011.01430.x

McLinden, M., Douglas, G., Cobb, R., Hewett, R. and Ravenscroft, J. (2016). 'Access to learning' and 'learning to access': Analysing the distinctive role of specialist teachers of children and young people with vision impairments in facilitating curriculum access through an ecological systems theory, *British Journal of Visual Impairment*, 34(2): 177–95. https://doi.org/10.1177/0264619616643180

McLinden, M., Douglas, G., Hewett, R., Cobb, R. and Lynch, P. (2017). Facilitating participation in education: The distinctive role of the specialist teacher in supporting learners with vision impairment in combination with severe and profound and multiple learning difficulties, *Journal of Blindness Innovation and Research*, 7(2). Available at: https://nfb.org/images/nfb/publications/jbir/jbir17/jbir070203.html [accessed 5 April 2022].

McLinden, M., Ravenscroft, J., Douglas, G., Cobb, R. and Hewett, R. (2017). The significance of specialist teachers of learners with visual impairments as agents of change: Examining personnel preparation in the United Kingdom through a bioecological systems theory, *Journal of Visual Impairment & Blindness*, 111(6): 569–84. https://doi.org/10.1177/0145482X1711100607

Meadows, S. (2004). Models of cognition in childhood: Metaphors, achievements and problems, in H. Daniels and A. Edwards (eds) *The Routledge Falmer Reader in Psychology of Education*. Routledge, pp. 135–83.

Meshcheryakov, A. (1979). *Awakening to Life* (trans. K. Judelson). Progress Publishers. Original work published 1974.

Miles, B. (1999). *Remarkable Conversations: A Guide to Developing Meaningful Communication with Children and Young Adults who are Deafblind*. Perkins School for the Blind.

Miles, B. (2000). *Literacy for Persons Who are Deaf-blind*, DB-LINK fact sheet. Available at: https://eric.ed.gov/?id=ED442215 [accessed 4 April 2022].

Miller, O.L. (2001). Multisensory environments: The use of interactive technology in effective pedagogy with learners who have severe and complex forms of special educational needs. Doctoral thesis, Institute of Education, University College London. Available at: https://discovery.ucl.ac.uk/id/eprint/10019803 [accessed 10 June 2022].

Miller, O. and Hodges, L. (2005). Deafblindness, in A. Lewis and B. Norwich (eds) *Special Teaching for Special Children?: Pedagogies for Inclusion*. Open University Press, pp. 41–52.

Miller, O.L., Keil, S. and Cobb, R. (2005). *A Review of the Literature on Accessible Curricula, Qualifications and Assessment*. Disability Rights Commission (DRC). Available at: https://disability-studies.leeds.ac.uk/wp-content/uploads/sites/40/library/miller-Final-Report-May-2005.pdf [accessed 7 April 2022].

Miller, O., Keil, S. and Whitehead, D. (2008). *Is there Still a Role for Designated Visual Impairment (VI) Special Schools in the 21st Century?* Report funded by the Esme Fairbairn Foundation. Institute of Education, University College London.

Miller, O.L. and McLarty, M. (2000). Curricular frameworks, in S. Aitken, M. Buultjens, C. Clark, J.T. Eyre and L. Pease (eds) *Teaching Children who are Deafblind: Contact, Communication and Learning*. David Fulton Publishers, pp. 141–66.

Miller, O., Wall, K. and Garner, M. (2011). *Quality Standards: Delivery of Habilitation Training (Mobility and Independent Living Skills) for Children and Young People with Visual Impairment*. Available at: https://habilitationviuk.org.uk/wp-content/uploads/2015/11/National-quality-Standards-habilitation-training.pdf [accessed 1 March 2022].

Mintz, J. and Wyse, D. (2015). Inclusive pedagogy and knowledge in special education: Addressing the tension, *International Journal of Inclusive Education*, 19(11): 1161–71. doi: 10.1080/13603116.2015.1044203

Mitra, S. (2006). Capability approach and disability, *Journal of Disability Policy Studies*, 16(4): 236–47. https://doi.org/10.1177/10442073060160040501

Mittler, P. (2000). *Working Towards Inclusive Education: Social Contexts*. David Fulton Publishers.

Möller, K. and Danermark, B. (2007). Social recognition, participation, and the dynamic between the environment and personal factors of students with deafblindness, *American Annals of the Deaf*, 152(1): 42–55. Available at: www.jstor.org/stable/26234422 [accessed 20 June 2022].

Moss, K. (1993). Looking at self-stimulation in the pursuit of leisure or I'm okay, you have a mannerism, *P.S. News!!!*, 5(3). Available at: www.tsbvi.edu/resources/2584-looking-at-self-stimulation-in-the-pursuit-of-leisure-or-im-okay-you-have-a-mannerism [accessed 5 April 2022].

Moss, K. (1995). Teaching strategies and content modifications for the child with deaf-blindness, *A–Z to Deafblindness*. Available at: www.deafblind.com/strategi.html [accessed 4 April 2022].

Murdoch, H. (1997). Multi-sensory impairment, in H. Mason and S. McCall (eds) *Visual Impairment: Access to Education for Children and Young People*. David Fulton Publishers, pp. 355–65.

Murdoch, H., Gough, A., Boothroyd, E. and Williams, K. (2014). Adding scents to symbols: Using food fragrances with deafblind young people making choices at mealtimes, *British Journal of Special Education*, 41(3): 249–67. doi: 10.1111/1467-8578.12072

Murdoch, H., McMinn, R., Gopsill, S., McLinden, A. and Smith, G. (2009). *A Curriculum for Multisensory Impaired Children*. Victoria School Birmingham and Sense.

Nafstad, A. (1991). *Space of Interaction*. Nordic Staff Training Centre for Deafblind Services (NUD).

Naish, L., Bell, J. and Clunies-Ross, L. (2003). *Exploring Access: How to Audit your School Environment, Focusing on the Needs of Children who have Multiple Disabilities and Visual Impairment*. RNIB.

Nelson, C., Hyte, H.A. and Greenfield, R. (2016). Increasing self-regulation and classroom participation of a child who is deafblind, *American Annals of the Deaf*, 160(5): 496–509. Available at: www.jstor.org/stable/10.2307/26235241 [accessed 10 June 2022].

Nelson, C., van Dijk, J., Oster, T. and McDonnell, A. (2009). *Child Guided Strategies: The van Dijk Approach to Assessment*. American Printing House for the Blind.

Nind, M. (2008). Promoting the emotional well-being of people with profound and multiple learning difficulties: A holistic approach through intensive interaction, in J. Pawlyn and S. Carnaby (eds) *Profound Intellectual and Multiple Disabilities: Nursing Complex Needs*. Wiley-Blackwell, pp. 62–77.

Norwich, B. and Lewis, A. (2007). How specialised is teaching children with disabilities and difficulties?, *Journal of Curriculum Studies*, 39(2): 127–50. doi: 10.1080/00220270601161667

Nussbaum, M. (2004). *Hiding from Humanity: Disgust, Shame and the Law*. Princeton University Press.

Nussbaum, M. (2011). *Creating Capabilities: The Human Development Approach*. Belknap Press.

Ockelford, A. (2000). Music in the education of children with severe or profound learning difficulties: Issues in current UK provision, a new conceptual framework, and proposals for research, *Psychology of Music*, 28: 197–217.

Ockelford, A. (2008). *Music for Children and Young People with Complex Needs*. Oxford University Press.

Ockelford, A. and Park, K. (2002). *Objects of Reference*. RNIB.

Ockelford, A., Welch, G., Jewell-Gore, L., Cheng, E., Vogiatzoglou, A. and Himonides, E. (2011). Sounds of intent, phase 2: Gauging the music development of children with complex needs, *European Journal of Special Needs Education*, 26(2): 177–99. doi: 10.1080/08856257.2011.563606

Ockelford, A., Welch, G., Zimmermann, S. and Himonides, E. (2005). 'Sounds of intent': Mapping, assessing and promoting the musical development of children with profound and multiple learning difficulties, *International Congress Series*, 1282(2): 898–902. doi:10.1016/j.ics.2005.04.007

Odom, S.L., Peck, C.A., Hanson, M. et al. (1996). Inclusion at the preschool level: An ecological systems analysis, *Social Policy Report: Society for Research in Child Development*, 10(2–3): 18–30.

Odom, S.L., Vitztum, J., Wolery, R. et al. (2004). Preschool inclusion in the United States: A review of research from an ecological systems perspective, *Journal of Research in Special Educational Needs*, 4(1): 17–49. doi: 10.1111/J.1471-3802.2004.00016.x

Oliver, M. (1990). *The Politics of Disablement: A Sociological Approach*. Palgrave Macmillan.

Pagliano, P. (1999). *Multisensory Environments*. David Fulton Publishers.

Park, K. (2004). Interactive storytelling: From the Book of Genesis, *British Journal of Special Education*, 31(1): 16–23.

Pearlman, S. and Michaels, D. (2019). Hearing the voice of children and young people with a learning disability during the Educational Health Care Plan (EHCP), *Support for Learning*, 34(2): 148–61. doi: 10.1111/1467-9604.12245

Pease, L. (2000). Creating a communicating environment, in S. Aitken, M. Buultjens, C. Clark, J.T. Eyre and L. Pease (eds) *Teaching Children who are Deafblind: Contact, Communication and Learning*. David Fulton Publishers, pp. 35–82.

Petroff, J.G. (2001). *National Transition Follow-up Study of Youth Identified as Deafblind: Parent Perspectives*, NTAC Briefing Paper. The National Technical Assistance Consortium for Children and Young Adults who are Deaf-Blind. Available at: www.govinfo.gov/content/pkg/ERIC-ED465234/pdf/ERIC-ED465234.pdf [accessed 5 April 2022].

Pilling, R.F. and Little, S.M. (2020). Evaluation of the role of the colour tent in vision stimulation for children with complex disabilities and cerebral visual impairment: A feasibility study, *British Journal of Visual Impairment*, 38(1): 104–14. doi: 10.1177/0264619619871980

Porter, J., Miller, O.L. and Pease, L. (1997). *Curriculum Access for Deafblind Children*. Research Report No. 1. Department for Education and Employment and Sense.

Preece, D. and Zhao, Y. (2015). Multi-sensory storytelling: A tool for teaching or an intervention technique?, *British Journal of Special Education*, 42(4): 429–43. doi: 10.1111/1467-8578.12116

Reed, L. and Addis, C. (1996). Developing a concept of control, in N. Bozic and H. Murdoch (eds) *Learning Through Interaction: Technology and Children with Multiple Disabilities*. David Fulton Publishers, pp. 116–31.

Robertson, J. and Emerson, E. (2010). *Estimating the Number of People with Co-occurring Vision and Hearing Impairments in the UK*. Centre for Disability Research, Lancaster University.

Romer, L.T. and Haring, N.G. (1994). The social participation of students with deafblindness in educational settings, *Education and Training in Mental Retardation and Developmental Disabilities*, 29(2): 134–44.

Roos, C., Cramer-Wolrath, E. and Falkman, K.W. (2016). Intersubjective interaction between deaf parents/deaf infants during the infant's first 18 months, *Journal of Deaf Studies and Deaf Education*, 21(1): 11–22. doi: 10.1093/deafed/env034

Rose, S. (2011). Similarities and differences between autism and deafblindness – a review of the literature. Unpublished master's thesis, University of Birmingham.

Rowland, C. (2013). *Handbook: Online Communication Matrix*. Oregon Health and Science University.

Roy, A., McVilly, K.R. and Crisp, B.R. (2021). Working with deafblind people to develop a good practice approach, *Journal of Social Work*, 21(1): 69–87. doi: 10.1177/1468017319860216

Sahamkhadam, N. (2020). Effect of in-service training on teachers' attitudes towards inclusion: A systematic literature review. Master's thesis, Jönköping University. DIVA portal. Available at: www.diva-portal.org/smash/get/diva2:1449551/FULLTEXT01.pdf [accessed 10 June 2022].

Sen, A.K. (1985). *Commodities and Capabilities*. North-Holland.

Sense (1988). *The Breaking Through Report*. Sense.

Sense (2002). *Breaking Out: Opening the Community for Deafblind Children and Young People*. A Sense Campaign Report. Sense.

Sense (2004). *Local Authority Survey Results*. Sense.

Shakespeare, T. (2010). The social model of disability, in L.J. Davis (ed.) *The Disability Studies Reader*. Routledge, pp. 266–73.

Shakespeare, T., Watson, N. and Alghaib, O. (2017). Blaming the victim, all over again: Waddell and Aylward's biopsychosocial (bps) model of disability, *Critical Social Policy*, 37(1): 22–41. doi: 10.1177/0261018316649120

References

Simmons, B.R. and Watson, D.L. (2014). *The PMLD Ambiguity: Articulating the Lifeworlds of Children with Profound and Multiple Learning Disabilities*. Karnac.

Sirgy, J. (1986). A quality-of-life theory derived from Maslow's developmental perspective: 'Quality' is related to progressive satisfaction of a hierarchy of needs, lower order and higher, *American Journal of Economics and Sociology*, 45(3): 329–42. https://doi.org/10.1111/j.1536-7150.1986.tb02394.x

Slee, R. (2018). *Inclusive Education isn't Dead, it Just Smells Funny*. Routledge Focus.

Slee, R. (2019). Belonging in an age of exclusion, *International Journal of Inclusive Education*, 23(9): 909–22. doi: 10.1080/13603116.2019.1602366

Sobsey, D. and Wolf-Schein, E.D. (1996). Children with sensory impairments, in F.P. Orelove and D. Sobsey (eds) *Educating Children with Multiple Disabilities: A Transdisciplinary Approach*. Paul H. Brookes, pp. 440–50.

Solomons, S. (2005). Using aromatherapy massage to increase shared attention behaviours in children with autistic spectrum disorders and severe learning difficulties, *British Journal of Special Education*, 32(3): 127–37. https://doi.org/10.1111/j.0952-3383.2005.00385.x

Stalker, K. (1998). Some ethical and methodological issues in research with people with learning difficulties, *Disability & Society*, 13(1): 5–19. doi: 10.1080/09687599826885

Stillman, R. and Battle, C. (1985). *The Callier-Azusa scale (H) for the Assessment of Communicative Abilities*. University of Texas at Dallas.

Tadema, A.C., Vlaskamp, C. and Ruijssenaars, W. (2008). Implementation of a programme for students with profound intellectual and multiple disabilities in schools: Three case studies, *Education and Training in Developmental Disabilities*, 43(4): 529–40. Available at: www.jstor.org/stable/23879681 [accessed 10 June 2022].

Tavoulari, A., Zeza, M., Katsoulis, P., Zafeira, D. and Skaltsouni, A. (2013). The sense of olfaction and taste as a base of an educational project for blind and deaf blind students. Paper presented at the 2nd Pan-Hellenic Congress of Special Education: Dilemmas and Perspectives in Special Education, Athens, Greece.

Taylor, K. (2007). The participation of children with multi-sensory impairment in person-centred planning, *British Journal of Special Education*, 34(4): 204–11.

Taylor, K. and Preece, D. (2010). Using aspects of the TEACCH structured teaching approach with students with multiple disabilities and visual impairment: Reflections on practice, *British Journal of Visual Impairment*, 28(3): 244–59.

The Scottish Office (2004). *Community Care Services for People with a Sensory Impairment: An Action Plan*. Scottish Executive Publications.

UNCRPD (2006). *The United Nations Convention on the Rights of Persons with Disabilities*, 13 December. Available at: https://www.ohchr.org/en/instruments-mechanisms/instruments/convention-rights-persons-disabilities [accessed 10 June 2022].

UNESCO (2019). *N for Nose: State of the Education Report for India 2019: Children with Disabilities*. Available at: https://en.unesco.org/news/n-nose-state-education-report-india-2019-children-disabilities [accessed 10 June 2022].

UNESCO (2020). *Global Education Monitoring Report 2020: Inclusion and Education: All means All*. Available at: https://en.unesco.org/gem-report/report/2020/inclusion [accessed 10 June 2022].

UNICEF UK (1989). *The United Nations Convention on the Rights of the Child*. Available at: https://downloads.unicef.org.uk/wp-content/uploads/2010/05/UNCRC_PRESS-200910web.pdf?_ga=2.78590034.795419542.1582474737-1972578648.1582474737 [accessed 10 June 2022].

Van Der Putten, A., Reynders, K., Vlaskamp, C. and Nakken, H. (2005). A functionally focused curriculum for children with profound multiple disabilities: A goal analysis, *Journal of Applied Research in Intellectual Disabilities*, 17(2): 71–5.

References

Van Dijk, J. (1991). *Persons Handicapped by Rubella: Victors and Victims.* Swets and Zeitlinger.

Van Dijk, J. and Nelson, C. (1996). Syndromes, behavior, and educational intervention, *Deaf-Blind Perspectives*, 4(2): 1–9.

Van Dijk, J. and Nelson, C. (1998). History and change in the education of children who are deaf-blind since the rubella epidemic of the 1960s: Influence of methods developed in the Netherlands, *Deaf-blind Perspectives*, 5(2): 1–5.

Vervloed, M.P., Van Dijk, R.J., Knoors, H. and van Dijk, J.P. (2006). Interaction between the teacher and the congenitally deafblind child, *American Annals of the Deaf*, 151(3): 336–44. Available at: www.jstor.org/stable/10.2307/26234390 [accessed 10 June 2022].

Vygotsky, L.S. (1978). *Mind in Society: The Development of Higher Psychological Processes* (ed. M. Cole, V. John-Steiner, S. Scribner and E. Souberman). Harvard University Press.

Waddell, G. and Aylward, M. (2010). *Models of Sickness and Disability: Applied to Common Health Problems.* Royal Society of Medicine Press. Available at: www.webility.md/praxis/downloads/Models-of-Sickness-Disability-Waddell-and-Aylward-2010-2.pdf [accessed 5 April 2022].

Wadsworth, J. (1999). Raising the profile of deafblindness, *New Beacon by RNIB*, 83(972). Available at: www.deafblind.com/jwadswor.htm [accessed 21 May 2021].

Wall, K. and Robinson, C. (2022). Look who's talking: Eliciting the voice of children from birth to seven, *European Early Childhood Education Research Journal*, 30(1): 1–7. doi: 10.1080/1350293X.2022.2026276

Warnock, M. (2005). *Special Educational Needs: A New Look.* Philosophy of Education Society of Great Britain.

Warren, D.H. (1984). *Blindness and Early Childhood Development.* American Foundation for the Blind.

Webster, A. and Roe, J. (1998). *Children with Visual Impairments: Social Interaction, Language and Learning.* Routledge.

Welch, T.R. and Goetz, L. (1997). Issues and concerns related to inclusive education for students who are deaf-blind, *Deaf-Blind Perspectives*, 4(3): 1–6.

Wertsch, J.V. (1985). *Vygotsky and the Social Formation of Mind.* Harvard University Press.

Wittich, W., Nicholas, J. and Damen, S. (2021). Living with deafblindness during COVID-19: An international webinar to facilitate global knowledge translation, *British Journal of Visual Impairment*, [online preprint] 1–13. doi: 10.1177/02646196211002887

World Federation of the Deafblind (2018). *At Risk of Exclusion from CRPD and SDGs Implementation: Inequality and Persons with Deafblindness: Initial Global Report on the Situation and Rights of Persons with Deafblindness.* Available at: www.wfdb.eu/wp-content/uploads/2019/06/WFDB_complete_Final.pdf [accessed 10 June 2022].

World Health Organization (WHO) (2001). *International Classification of Functioning, Disability and Health ICF.* Available at: www.who.int/standards/classifications/international-classification-of-functioning-disability-and-health [accessed 10 June 2022].

Wright, R. (2020). Who is 'worthy'? Deaf-blind people fear that doctors won't save them from the coronavirus, *The New Yorker*, 28 April. Available at: 'www.newyorker.com/news/our-columnists/who-is-worthy-deaf-blind-people-fear-that-doctors-wont-save-them-from-the-coronavirus [accessed 10 June 2022].

Yin, R. (2014). *Case Study Research: Design and Methods*, 5th edn. SAGE. doi: 10.3138/cjpe.30.1.108

Index

access, 9, 19, 28, 34, 60-61, 71-73
accessibility, 22, 42, 95, 101
acoustics, 72
adaptations, 8, 23, 27, 42, 58, 60, 62, 71, 79, 90, 95, 97, 99, 102
   children's views, 85
   research interviews, 86
   tactile, 67, 69
Alternative and Augmentative Communication (AAC) systems, 27, 29, 39, 69, 97
anticipation, 59, 75, 76
aromatherapy massage, 35, 78
assessment, 19, 25, 58
   and co-morbidity, 37
   holistic, 38, 57
   methods, 5
   of communication, 26, 64-65
   of environmental barriers, 81
   of risks, 73
   research, 25, 32
   tools, 26, 32, 64
assistive technology, 27, 68, 101
Attachment, 18, 39, 40
   theory, 46, 47, 48, 51, 57, 100
Attention Deficit Hyperactivity Disorder (ADHD), 4, 95
Autistic Spectrum Disorder (ASD), 4, 25, 26, 27, 70, 83

Bandura, Albert, 48, 49
behaviourism, 39, 100
Bioecological Systems Theory (BST), 34, 43, 46, 52-53, 56-57, 80-81, 100
biopsychosocial model, 47, 56
body awareness, 22
Bowlby, John, 18, 47
Braille, 11, 19, 34, 64, 68, 72, 77
British Sign Language (BSL), 67, 68
Bronfenbrenner, 30, 34, 43, 52-53, 57
buddy system, 82
bullying, 57, 81-83

calendars, 75-76, 78
Callier-Azusa Scale 'H', 64

Capability Approach, 47, 56-57, 100
case studies, 15, 18, 23, 31-32, 35, 38, 90-95, 99
challenging behaviour, 22, 26, 40, 46, 49
CHARGE, 3, 32-33
child-centred planning, 25
children's voices, 10, 36, 84-87, 99
choice making, 27, 35, 78-79
clutter and noise, 4, 35, 72
co-active movement, 18, 60, 65-66
cochlear implants, 78
cognitive development, 16-17, 45, 51, 90
cognitive skills, 59, 60, 61
colour contrast, 72, 91
communication
   and environment, 77
   complex needs, 18, 27, 64, 78, 97, 99
   development, 19-20, 58, 60, 64, 65-70
   dictionary, 26
   functional, 27
   human aids to, 68
   humour and laughter, 28
   intentional, 64, 65, 66
   interface, 27
   interventions, 19-20, 24-26, 95
   matrix, 64
   means, 11, 49, 51, 63, 65, 102
   methods, 25-26, 33, 44, 63-69, 102
   natural, 18
   non-verbal, 40-41, 66-67
   parent-teacher, 19, 23, 30, 52, 73, 83, 84, 89
   partner, 22, 24, 26, 28, 40, 44, 45, 49, 51, 55, 65, 67
   passport, 26, 27
   portfolio, 22
   potential, 17, 64
   presymbolic (also non-symbolic), 65, 68
   preverbal, 70
   receptive and expressive, 27, 28, 33, 40, 60, 63, 68
   repertoire, 28
   skills, 39, 60, 69, 70
   strategies for, 63, 65-66
   style, 38

122 Index

symbolic, 65-67
systems, 16, 20, 23, 26, 66
teacher-support staff, 29-30
technological aids to, 68, 78,
unintentional, 64-66
concept development, 66, 76,
cooperative learning, 23, 82
Covid-19, 42
cues, 55, 60, 65-66, 76,
cultural
   beliefs, 8
   context, 18, 98
   factors, 5
curriculum, 90
   developmental or modified, 19, 63
   national, 19,
   specialised, 37, 38,
   subjects, 79

deafblindness, *see* Multisensory Impairment
devices, 26, 27, 31, 68, 101
diagnosis, 3, 4, 32,
differentiation, 23-24, 81-82
dramatherapy, 28-29
drawings, 66
Dual Sensory Impairment (DSI), 1, 4, 6, 13, 102

Ecological Systems Theory (EST), 30, 52
Education Health and Care Plan (EHCP), 6, 29, 87
empathy, 40
employment, 5
expectations, of adults, 75-76
exploratory studies, 20
equipment, 79-80

fading, 75
fingerspelling, 14-15, 67
flexibility, 27, 32, 38, 40, 86, 88-89, 90, 99
fragrances, 35, 78
Fraiberg, Selma, 54
frustration, 49, 74
functioning, 41, 47, 56-57
   social and emotional, 60, 62, 81
functional vision and/or hearing, 19, 77
funding, 7, 9, 31, 42, 103

gesture, 27-28, 53-54, 65-67
Girma, Heben, 72, 77, 101

Global Education Monitoring Report (GEM), 7, 9
global North, 6-10, 42, 98
global South, 6-10, 42, 98-100

habilitation, 72-73
hand-over-hand, 77
hand-under-hand, 77
hearing aids, 78, 93, 94
hearing impairment, 28, 54

idiosyncratic
   behaviours, 44, 45, 68
   cues, 65
   sign systems, 67
imitation, 16, 48, 61
incidental learning, 16, 48, 61
inclusive education, 6-9, 84
   attitudes to, 9, 10
   challenges, 7
   definition of, 7-8
   in the global South, 98
   teacher preparation for, 10, 102
independence, 16, 18, 23, 27, 30, 32, 34, 37, 38, 59, 60, 62, 71-73, 79,
   skills, 44, 45, 73, 91
Individual Education Plan (IEP), 81
insecurity, sense of, 41, 45, 48, 58
intensive interaction, 26, 69-70, 97
interactive story-telling, 31
interactive technology, 31, 59, 79
International Classification of Functioning (ICF) model, 47, 56-57, 100
interpreter, 68
intervenor, 51, 68
intervention, 11, 14, 20-21, 34, 39, 81-82, 97-98
   auditory verbal, 28
   early, 28
   musical, 33-34
   reading, 40
   studies, 10, 21-24, 26-27, 31, 35-36, 40
   tactile, 20, 35
isolation, 22, 27, 30, 41, 45

joint activity, 16, 18, 51

Keller, Helen, 14-15
keyworker, 35
kinaesthetic stimulation, 79

Index

landmarks, 72
language
  body, 77
  development, 28, 38, 44
  input, 67
  second, 60, 91
  skills, 60
  spoken, 67
  therapist, 26,
  written, 68
large print, 68
leading, 76
learned helplessness, 45, 49
learning styles, 32
Learning Support Assistants (LSAs), 29
leisure time, 22, 24, 30
Leontiev, Alexei, 17-18
lighting and shade, 37, 72
lip-reading, 28, 67, 86, 92, 93
lip-speaker, 68
literacy, 34, 39-41, 59, 76
Low Vision Aids (LVAs), 78

Marx, Karl, 17-18
Maslow, Abraham, 100-101
matrix skill, 75
medical model, 47, 48, 81
memory, 38, 48, 59, 75, 78
Meshcheryakov, Alexander, 13, 15-18, 51, 100
mobility and orientation, 44-46, 59-60, 72-73
modelling, 16, 23, 50, 58, 76
models of disability, 47, 52, 57, 98
Moon, 19, 34, 68
motivation, 36, 38, 45, 61, 78, 80
  extrinsic, 45
motor skills
  gross and fine, 27, 61-62, 71, 129
Multiple Disabilities and Vision Impairment (MDVI), 6, 13, 26, 34, 35-36
Multisensory Environment (MSE), 31, 79
Multisensory Impairment (MSI)
  and overlapping labels, 13-14
  awareness of self, 17, 35, 44
  causes, 3
  co-morbidity, 4
  definition, 1, 2-4, 5, 99-100
  raising awareness about, 23, 82, 99-101
  terminology, 3-4, 6, 14, 25, 98, 99
  types of, 2-3
multisensory stories, 31-32, 97
musical development, 33

object cues, 65
objects of reference, 19, 26, 27, 60, 66, 75
observation, 17, 64, 85, 87-89
  informal, 27, 32
  matrix, 27
  semi-structured, 30
  skills, 16, 48, 61
  studies, 25, 26, 27, 31, 33-35, 38-40, 85
  qualitative, 18, 28, 88-89
obstacles and risks, 72, 73
olfactory, 35, 79
one-to-one lessons, 19, 23, 27, 81-82
oralism, 28

pace, 74-75
peer
  attitudes, 82
  interaction, 20-23, 29-30, 39-40, 51, 61, 80-82, 88
  networks, 22, 82
  relationships, 21-24, 61-62, 80-83
Perkins School for the Blind, 14-15, 33
personal identifiers, 76
physical development, 60
physical proximity, 42, 44, 67
Piaget, Jean, 18, 100
pictures, 39, 65, 66, 77
Picture Exchange Communication System (PECS), 26, 69
play, 22, 28, 37-38, 40
prompting, 59, 62, 75, 76, 86, 100
proprioception, 60-61

repetition, 49, 59, 61, 62, 66, 75, 100
repetitive experiences, 59, 74
residential provision or schools, 9
residual vision and/or hearing, 5, 46, 55, 69
resonance, 18, 66
resources, 5, 8, 9, 11, 12, 29, 31, 34, 40, 58, 60, 79, 103
rights, 5, 84
risk assessment, 73
routines, 33, 35, 59, 60, 75, 90
rehabilitation, 72-73

Royal National Institute for the Blind (RNIB), 5, 6, 72, 73
Rubella, 3, 18, 94

Salamanca Statement, 7, 10, 102
scaffolding, 17-18, 50, 59, 62, 65, 75
school placement
  mainstream, 8-9, 19, 20, 21, 24, 29, 31-32, 39, 40, 62-63, 83, 97-98
  parental views about, 8, 22-23
  special, 9, 19, 21, 29, 31-32, 39, 62-63, 83, 97-98
security, sense of, 74, 75, 76, 78
self-awareness, 16-17, 35, 44,
self-care skills, 16, 100
self-esteem, 34, 45, 48, 85
self-harm, 49
self-regulation, 33, 40, 71
SEN/D Code of Practice (CoP), 84
Sense, 5, 18-19, 30
Sensory and Social Deprivation Theories, 48-50, 100
sensory awareness, 62, 71
sensory input, 4, 17-18, 46, 49-50, 59, 61, 77, 80
sensory processing or integration issues, 4
Severe or Profound Multiple Learning Disabilities (S/PMLD), 6, 13, 25, 29-30, 33, 57
sign languages, 67
signage and displays, 72
signing, 19, 67, 77
signs, 27, 54, 65, 67
Single Sensory Impairment (SSI), 4, 6, 53, 54, 77
smell, 35, 44, 55, 60, 77-78, 97
social and emotional development, 40, 45-57, 61, 80-83
social inclusion, 30, 34, 48, 53, 80-83, 86
Social Learning Theory, 48-50, 100
social model, 47, 50
social network analysis, 21
social participation, 20-23, 30, 82, 101
social skills, 22, 23, 30, 45, 49-50, 61, 81
socialization, 23, 30, 45-46, 81-83
sociocultural theory, 50-52, 57, 100
space, awareness of, *see* concept development
Special Educational Needs/Disabilities (SEN/D), 4, 53, 102

stereotypic behaviours, 46
stigma, 46, 98
strategies, 11, 23, 25, 33, 40, 44, 59-63, 73, 75
  auditory, 78-79
  children's voice, 84-87
  haptic, 20, 34, 77-78, 54-55
  oflactory, 35, 54-55
  learning, 48-50
  meta-strategies, 60
  teaching, 19, 82
  visual, 26-27, 35-36, 78-79
structuring the environment, 26, 61, 71-72
Sullivan, Anne, 14, 15
Sustainable Development Goals (SDGs), 7, 100
switches, 26, 31, 68, 79-80

tactile
  books, 80
  cues, 44, 76
  input, 72
  objects, 66
  pictures, 66, 77
  schedules, 27
  sense, 48, 95
  sign language, 86
Tadoma, 67
tangible objects, 27
tangible symbols, 39, 41, 64
task analysis, 75
taste, 44, 77-78, 97
teacher training, 7, 10, 23, 80, 101-103
teaching style, 59-62, 73-76
time, awareness of, *see* concept development
timetables, 26
touch, 28, 35, 40, 42, 44, 54-55, 67, 68, 77-78
touchscreens, 79
Treatment and Education of Autistic and related Communication-handicapped Children (TEACCH), 26-27
triangulation, 25, 64, 89, 99
trust, 39, 61, 64, 68, 74, 85

UN Convention on the Rights of the Child (UNCRC), 84
UNESCO, 7, 9

United Nations Convention on the Rights of Persons with Disabilities (UNCRPD), 7, 9, 10, 73, 84, 102
Universal Design (UD), 71
Universal Design for Learning (UDL), 40, 71, 102
Usher, 3, 39, 63, 101

van Dijk, Jan, 18, 39, 46, 47, 51, 61, 65-66
vestibular sense, 60-61

vision impairment, 6, 8, 9, 54, 67, 72,
vocalisation, 27-28, 40, 53, 65, 66
Vygotsky, Lev, 16-18, 50-51

World Federation of the Deafblind Report, 5, 9, 11, 100, 103
World Health Organisation (WHO), 47, 56

Zone of Proximal Development (ZPD), 17, 18, 50

www.ingramcontent.com/pod-product-compliance
Lightning Source LLC
Chambersburg PA
CBHW052025290426
44112CB00014B/2382